CRAFT COCKTAILS

CRAFT COCKTAILS

SEASONALLY INSPIRED DRINKS AND SNACKS FROM OUR SIPPING ROOM

GEOFF DILLON AND WHITNEY RORISON

of Dillon's Small Batch Distillers

PENGUIN

an imprint of Penguin Canada, a division of Penguin Random House Canada Limited

Canada • USA • UK • Ireland • Australia • New Zealand • India • South Africa • China

First published 2019

www.penguinrandomhouse.ca

Library and Archives Canada Cataloguing in Publication

Title: Craft cocktails : seasonally inspired drinks and snacks from our sipping room / Geoff Dillon and Whitney Rorison.
Names: Dillon, Geoff, author | Rorison, Whitney, author
Identifiers: Canadiana (print) 20190045140 | Canadiana (ebook) 20190045159 | ISBN 978-0-7352-3529-8 (softcover) | ISBN 978-0-7352-3530-4 (PDF)
Subjects: LCSH: Cocktails. | LCSH: Appetizers. | LCGFT: Cookbooks.
Classification: LCC TX951 .D55 2019 | DDC 641.87/4—dc23

Book design by Five Seventeen
Cover design by Five Seventeen
Cover images and interior photography by Nataschia Wielink Photography

Printed and bound in China

10 9 8 7 6 5 4 3 2

Penguin
Random House
PENGUIN CANADA

TO OUR PARTNERS IN LIFE,
IN DISTILLING, AND IN COCKTAIL MIXING

Contents

INTRODUCTION

I knew from an early age that I wanted to forge my own path. By the time I was in my early twenties, I had finished a degree in biology and economics and was looking for a career that could use both. You might be surprised to learn that distilling immediately came to mind.

My interest in distilling had humble—and not so palatable—beginnings. I began dabbling in home-brew beer, and our student rental made its own house wine. It was terrible. Ask my wife. But that didn't stop us from drinking it by the gallon and serving it proudly to our unsuspecting guests. In the end, we knew our fermented grape drink was never going to make it beyond the doors of our dorm, so my engineer roommate and I decided to try our hand at something a little different. We learned the physics and mechanics required for building a still so that we could make our own spirits, and what started out as a fun experiment quickly turned into serious business.

This first foray into making distilled spirits awakened an appreciation of rare and fine spirits that was fostered by my father. When I would return home for the summer during university, we'd sit in his living room and taste and review the newest additions to his spirit collection. In his extensive travels as a chemistry professor, he collected countless one-of-a-kind whiskies from Scotland, elusive sloe gins from the United Kingdom, incredible eaux-de-vie from France, and unique liquors from all over the globe. When he worked with graduate students from around the world, he always had one requirement of them—that they bring him a bottle of an unusual spirit from their home country to help him build his collection. I remember sampling a ginseng spirit with the root of the plant floating in the bottle. Now, ten years later, I can still taste it. In many ways, my dad sowed the seed for a father-son duo to take the craft distilling world by storm.

Suddenly, I wanted to learn everything I could about spirits—the styles, the ingredients, the equipment. But mostly, I wanted to make them. The spark had been lit and I knew distilling would become my lifelong passion. The more I learned about distilling, both formally and informally, the clearer it became: distilling, to me, was so much more exciting than making beer or wine. There was so much freedom with distilling. You could take merlot wine and distill it into gin. A distillery can transform an alcohol-based liquid (beer or wine) into a clear 95% alcohol with no flavour that can then be used to craft flavourful gins, vodkas, liqueurs, or whatever else you dream up. It was this freedom and the possibilities for exploration that drew me in.

The idea of starting a craft distillery was daunting, but my bigger fear was waking up in twenty years only to realize I had missed my calling. I knew this was my time, so I decided to go all in. I earned a Master Distiller certificate from the Institute of Brewing and Distilling, in the United Kingdom, and gained hands-on experience working in craft distilleries in Scotland and the United States. I soaked up all the distilling techniques and know-how I could. By the time my tour was over, the only thing I needed was a distillery.

My timing couldn't have been better. In the 2000s, small distilleries were beginning to pop up in greater numbers across North America. Small family-run distilleries in other parts of the world had been making spirits for generations, but the idea of pure experimentation—of creating anything you want from whatever ingredients are on hand—was a newer one.

I spent some time getting to know the industry and sampling some of the amazing spirits coming out of distilleries in California, Colorado, Utah, and Washington, and I could feel the momentum building. Consumers expected more from the products they were going to put into their bodies, and there was a clear difference between the quality of what the big companies were producing and what smaller operations could achieve with more care and attention. These consumers cared more than ever where the ingredients came from and who was making the product. They were also looking for a real connection to the producer, an honest story. A movement was beginning to take hold, and there was no way that I wasn't going to be a part of it.

At the time, I was newly engaged, and my fiancée's father, Gary Huggins, was paramount in making my dream a reality. He is a lifelong entrepreneur and dreamer himself. Lucky for me, he liked my dream, and he also believed that I could make it a reality. He would listen to my crazy ideas about making booze and not only would he take me seriously, but he would go on to convince me and the rest of the team that starting a craft distillery was possible—and that we could make it successful. After some years of hard work, the distillery began to emerge in brick, mortar, and copper. Dillon's Small Batch Distillers was born.

As we quickly approached time to open the distillery, we knew that we needed someone to help direct the hospitality side of the business, an area we had no experience in. We were lucky enough to meet Whitney Rorison. She had years of expertise under her belt in hospitality in the Niagara area, having helped in the successful openings of many wineries and even a brewery. She came on board in late 2012 to help guide us and build the visitor experience side of the distillery, and has grown to do so much more. It's thanks to Whitney that you're able to enjoy this book, because she helped write it.

In the evolution of the distillery, my father has remained an important player. While my dad spent his career studying freshwater lakes as a renowned environmental scientist and chemist, his passion has always been spirits. Today, he lives on a beautiful ten-acre hobby farm just outside Bowmanville, Ontario. He grows all kinds of botanicals, herbs, and fruit, and has become the "mad scientist" behind our flavours. His lab is his lair where tinctures are tweaked and botanicals are boiled to create the lush spirits we sell today.

THE INGREDIENTS

Ingredients play the single largest role in our spirits—more than our team, more than the equipment, more than the story. We don't forget that. The search for quality ingredients is also what led us to our home in the Niagara region of southern Ontario.

Being situated in a rural location in Beamsville—the epicentre of Ontario's fruit belt—gives us a strong connection with our local farmers and their crops. Each of our ingredients is sourced within 100 kilometres of our distillery. With Canada's climate varying from temperate to downright frigid, there are only a few small pockets in the country with the warmth and lime-rich soil that can sustain delicate stone fruits and nurture hardy but complex grape varietals. Niagara is one of these special spots—and one of the best.

We use local grapes as the base for our crisp, clean-tasting vodka and our full-bodied Unfiltered Gin 22. Fresh Niagara fruits, including strawberries, cherries, and plums, have given us the ability to create flavourful and whimsical gin liqueurs, such as Dillon's Rose Gin, Cherry Gin, and Strawberry Gin, among others. As you will see, these fruits (and more!) play a role in many of our playful cocktails. Equally important is nearby Brant County, which supplies fresh, flavourful rye grain to bakeries all over Ontario. Since we started distilling, Brant County has supplied all the rye we use in our whiskies.

Above all, the character of a spirit comes down to how well its ingredients are expressed. We believe there's beauty in simplicity. Whether we're making vodka, gin, whisky, or a liqueur, our goal is to show off the ingredients that go into making that spirit.

The same is true of cocktails. If we were going to achieve any success, we knew we had to craft spirits that bartenders wanted to use. The culture around drinking cocktails has changed in recent years. Many bartenders are bringing back the classics, but many are also crafting their own distinctive drinks. The quality of the spirits that go into a cocktail goes a long way in shaping the flavour of the finished drink.

To celebrate a wealth of flavours and ingredients, as well as the amazing talent of barkeeps in cities near and far, we created the Dillon's Cocktail Cup. The Dillon's Cocktail Cup is unlike any other cocktail competition out there. We designed it to be more inclusive—an event where not only the judges have an opportunity to taste and evaluate the cocktails, but the guests do too. With each round hosted at a different bar, bartenders from all over the country come together to compete head to head until we've narrowed it down to just one winner. Cocktails are judged on their flavour, but the bartenders are also graded on how they work behind the bar and entertain the crowd while making drinks. Each year, bartenders surprise us with the array of ingredients they bring to the table and the exciting ways their creative combinations bring out the nuanced flavours of our handcrafted spirits. In many ways, our cocktails take their inspiration from the ingenious barkeeps we've seen compete year after year—and some of their creations are featured in this book.

I hope that you enjoy reading through these recipes and take pride in crafting them in your home as much as we enjoyed creating and drinking them ourselves here at Dillon's.

THE PROCESS

Our philosophy has always been to combine the freshest, highest-quality local ingredients with old-school distilling techniques and new-school equipment. This has led us to build bespoke equipment to craft our distinctive spirits. With our diverse equipment and its wide-ranging capacities, we can produce larger quantities of spirits while still doing everything in-house. Even as demand increases, we continue to distill spirits in our way—grain-to-glass with a hands-on process every step of the way.

Blending traditional with modern distilling equipment, we currently have a team of three stills, affectionately nicknamed Carl Sr., Carl Jr., and Beaut. I've been known to go on at length about each of them and treat them like family members (again, just ask my wife), but here I will try to give a concise description of our equipment and explain why we use it. It's always hard when you're so passionate about steel and copper to whittle it down to a few sentences!

CARL SR. AND CARL JR.

Both Carl Sr. and Carl Jr. were made by the legendary German still builders Carl. These stills are the heart of our operation. (Both were delivered shortly after I returned from my honeymoon. Talk about an exciting homecoming!) Carl Sr. does the lion's share of the distilling, with its large 2100-gallon capacity. It is a unique hybrid mash tank and pot still and the first of its kind in the world. Unlike most stills, which ferment grains and distill spirits in separate tanks, Carl Sr. serves as both a mash tank, to convert the starch in the grain into sugar for fermenting, and a pot still, distilling the spirit one batch at a time. Carl Jr. is a modern copper pot still with a classic look. With a 120-gallon capacity, this still is perfect for finishing off the work of Carl Sr. with more refinement and precision. Rising above it are twenty-three copper plates with trays that capture and condense the evaporated alcohol from the pot still. At that stage we are able to control the final percentage of alcohol in the liquid and to maintain the flavour of our spirits.

BEAUT

Beaut is a modern marvel of distilling (complete with an integrated touch screen) in a surprisingly compact package made by Headframe Spirits Manufacturing in Butte, Montana. And boy, oh boy, is it a beaut. Beaut helps us fulfill our goal of blending old and new distilling techniques and stills, while allowing superior control and monitoring, which results in our distinct, high-quality small-batch spirits. Beaut distills many of our base alcohols in a single distillation to 95% alcohol by volume (ABV), resulting in clean bases for our gins and vodkas. This frees up Carl Sr. and Carl Jr. to be the powerhouses behind our twice pot-distilled rye whisky and brandies. They also carry out the fourth and final run of our gins, when they are vapour distilled with botanicals.

USING THIS BOOK THROUGH THE SEASONS

Situated in a thriving farming community, Dillon's benefits from each season's harvest, with each fresh ingredient we receive adding seasonal flair to our many spirits. Remaining true to the way we do things, we have divided the recipes in *Craft Cocktails* into sections for Spring, Summer, Fall, and Winter, to use the best ingredients each season has to offer. At the end of each section of seasonally focused cocktail recipes—some traditional, some completely modern—we have included our favourite cocktail-inspired snacks. Rosemary Maple Pecans (page 179), Spring Pea Crostini (page 76), or Gourmet Grown-Up Popcorn, Two Ways (page 132) are good accompaniments to any cocktail. Other recipes, such as Strawberry Gin Shaved Ice (page 127) and Warm Potato Salad with DSB Vinaigrette (page 79), incorporate spirits and bitters into plates you can invite your friends to nibble on at your next gathering.

At the distillery, we like to put our feet up and enjoy a Rhubarb Sour (page 43) in late spring, and in the summer, we always make the most of the Niagara Gold peach harvest by crafting a batch of Summer Sangria (page 103). When cooler breezes come our way in the fall, we shift gears and sip on classics like a Boulevardier (page 206) or a Spiced Pear Fizz (page 168). And because we know that you will want to share your favourite cocktails with friends, we have included some large-batch recipes that are meant to be enjoyed with a group. No matter how you choose to savour our favourite handcrafted cocktail recipes, we think you will enjoy making your way through each season with a different cocktail (or two!) in hand.

STOCKING YOUR HOME BAR

There are some wonderful small-batch artisanal spirits available nowadays. Between the spirits that we produce at Dillon's and others crafted by talented distillers around the world, the selection of one-of-a-kind spirits to offer variety to your home bar cart has never been better. In addition, there are some staple spirits everyone should have in their home bar that are produced by larger distilleries around the world. Below, we've compiled a list of the spirits we feel every home bar should have on hand. In addition to the core spirits that you will use more regularly, we've listed some bottles that may take longer to finish, but we promise they will come in handy. The great thing about spirits and liqueurs is that they don't really have a best before date. With the exception of fortified wines, which will last for about three months when stored in the fridge after they've been opened, these classic bar staples will last.

BASE SPIRITS

The following spirits form the base of almost every drink we mix, and of many that don't appear in the pages of this book.

VODKA

Typically crafted using grain or potato, vodka tends to be as neutral a spirit as they come. It is used in a wide range of classic cocktails, including the Dillon's Caesar (page 120), Moscow Mule (page 112), and Classic Martini (page 39).

DILLON'S RYE VODKA

Our more traditional grain-based vodka is crafted using a 100% Ontario rye grain base. Fermented and distilled to a neutral spirit, this vodka offers a clean and crisp taste—the perfect partner for all your go-to vodka cocktails.

DILLON'S METHOD 95

Our locally driven take on the classic spirit is crafted using 100% Niagara wine grapes. With a touch of grape flavour and natural sweetness present on the finish, it is less neutral than the classic style, and also a little cheeky. Even though this spirit may have a bit more character than others, it still works well in all the classic vodka-based cocktails.

GIN

Often referred to as the world's first flavoured vodka, gin is made by adding herbs and botanicals to a neutral spirit base. The botanicals range so vastly that you may never come across two gins that taste the same. As long as juniper (which gives gin its pine-tree aroma and taste) is the main botanical used, you've got yourself a gin. With so many different styles of gin available—from London Dry (a more traditional, juniper-forward style), to Genever (distilled from malt wine and sometimes aged in wood), to Old Tom (a slightly sweeter take on a London Dry gin), to New Western (a more aromatic style)—it is a good idea to have a few variations on hand depending on the styles you prefer and what kinds of cocktails you are looking to make. Throughout the book you will find many cocktails made with gin, with some of our favourites being the Spiced Pear Fizz (page 168), Bee's Knees (page 56), and of course the Classic Gin and Tonic (page 35). For some recipes we recommend using dry gin, but where we don't specify, go with your favourite.

DILLON'S UNFILTERED GIN 22

Our original New Western–style gin is made from a base of 100% local wine grapes and vapour distilled through twenty-two botanicals. It is floral and fresh, with an impressively smooth mouthfeel thanks to the grape base. The mix of botanicals includes many local floral notes, including homegrown lavender and hibiscus. Our distilling process is designed to keep in all the flavour, resulting in a slightly cloudy gin when proofed or chilled in a cocktail.

DILLON'S DRY GIN 7

A traditional dry style gin made by vapour distilling through juniper and just six other botanicals. This classic gin is made from a base of 100% Ontario rye grain. It has a more pronounced juniper and citrus flavour and is finished to a higher proof, which makes it the perfect gin to use in a Classic Martini (page 39).

DILLON'S FRUIT AND LIQUEUR-STYLE GINS

Our infused liqueur-style gins are all crafted using our Dry Gin 7 as the base. Each is then steeped with its own recipe of ingredients, sweetened with organic cane sugar, and proofed to 30% to 35% alcohol by volume (ABV). Our Rose Gin pairs rosehips and rose petals to steep in the gin base. The result is a rich flavour profile of floral notes, cinnamon, and an almost tea-like herbal quality. In the summer, we use sour cherries to make our tart-tasting Cherry Gin with a pronounced juniper finish. Local strawberries bring the taste of a stewed strawberry jam to our Strawberry Gin, and our Plum Gin is created by hand pressing and macerating different plum varieties in the Dry Gin 7 before it is barrel-aged in first-fill bourbon casks for one to two years, giving it the taste of a sweet, fruit-forward whisky. These spirits are able to hold up well as the main spirit component of a drink because of their higher than normal alcohol content, but they also marry well with something like a traditional gin or vodka in a cocktail. With so many handcrafted spirits available on the market, have fun creating your own unique combinations.

WHISKY

Whisky is typically made from a blend of different grains, usually corn, wheat, barley, and rye, with each grain contributing distinct flavour profiles to the finished spirit. All whisky is aged in oak casks, but the aging time will vary depending on where the whisky is produced. Most Canadian whiskies are generally made of some combination of corn, wheat, barley, and rye, and in many cases they are lighter in flavour and have a smoother finish than other aged grain spirits such as Scotch and bourbon. Since about 2010, distillers in Canada have shifted from mostly corn-based spirits toward using rye grain more often, and it has become common to see rye-forward spirits. As defined by law in Canada, "rye whisky," "whisky," and "Canadian whisky" are all acceptable terms for a barrel-aged grain spirit, although very few distillers were using 100% rye in their recipe. So long as the finished spirit looks and tastes like whisky, was aged for at least three years in oak casks, and was crafted fully in Canada, what it is made from is up to the distiller.

The reputation of Canadian whisky has come a long way in recent years, and because Canadian distillers now use more rye as their base grain, we are now crafting some of the finest whiskies in the world. Many of the world's most classic cocktails are made with whisky as their base, among them the Whisky Sour (page 44), Mint Julep (page 64), and the Manhattan (page 151).

Bourbon is a style of American whisky crafted in the United States, with a recipe of at least 51% corn that is aged in new oak casks. Scotch is distilled and aged in Scotland and is composed mainly of barley. Both offer characteristic flavour profiles thanks to their differing mash bills and aging conditions.

DILLON'S THE WHITE RYE

This purist's rye is handcrafted from 100% Ontario-grown rye but is not aged in wood, allowing the true flavours of the grain to shine through. Because rye grain has a spicier flavour profile and an almost tequila-like quality, it works quite well in a Margarita (page 60). This spirit works well in a number of other great cocktails, but they are not your classics.

DILLON'S RYE WHISKY

Crafted using 100% Ontario rye, this grain-to-glass spirit has been aged in a variety of different casks for a minimum of three years. We age in new Ontario oak, new American oak, and first-fill bourbon casks.

DILLON'S RYE 1 WHISKY

Every year, we release one rye whisky cask as a single offering. It is a cask that we have earmarked as one of our favourites and, after 36 to 50 months of aging in new Ontario oak, we do not proof it down before we bottle it. The result is 57.2% alcohol, distilled from 100% Ontario rye grain—a sipping whisky that you can enjoy neat or on the rocks.

TEQUILA

This spirit is crafted using blue agave grown in Mexico. With so much variety in this category of spirit, it may take some time to find your favourite brand. Tequila is the base for classic cocktails like the Margarita (page 60) and a Mexican-style Paloma (page 116).

RUM

Rum is made from distilled sugar cane or sugar cane by-products like molasses and then, in many cases, aged in barrels. A wide variety of white rums and spiced rums are also readily available. White rum is the less aged counterpart of dark rum and tends to have a slightly sweeter taste. Spiced rum has a blend of spices added, typically after aging for at least one year, giving it more character. There is a wide range of rum available on liquor store shelves, so do some research to determine which one will best suit your taste. Try using your favourite aged rum in our Eggnog recipe (page 194).

ABSINTHE

This anise-flavoured spirit gets its name from the wormwood or *Artemisia Absinthium* plant it is made from. It has a higher ABV percentage than most other spirit types; the ABV for most absinthe ranges from 50% to 75%. Because of absinthe's high alcohol content and intense anise flavour and aroma, not many cocktails make use of it as the main spirit, but you will find it in classics like the Sazerac (page 218) and Corpse Reviver #2 (page 217). More commonly, it is served in the traditional absinthe service (page 201), often with a water fountain and sugar cubes.

DILLON'S ABSINTHE

Absinthe can be crafted in any number of ways, but ours is made with fresh wormwood, lemon balm, and hyssop grown in the distillery garden, in addition to traditional botanicals such as fennel and star anise. It is made by vapour distilling botanicals with a rye-grain spirit base as well as steeping or maceration with botanicals and fresh grapefruit peel.

LIQUEURS

To be classified as a liqueur, some addition of sweetness to the spirit in the form of sugar is required. Liqueurs make wonderful additions to cocktails but aren't always the most dominant ingredient. They are amazing modifiers or sweeteners, and are added to drinks to yield a more balanced and complex cocktail.

LIMONCELLO AND ORANGECELLO

These traditional Italian lemon- or orange-flavoured liqueurs are great on their own as an aperitivo or mixed in cocktails.

DILLON'S LIMONCELLO

Some varieties of limoncello tend to be rather intense or sweet, so we took a different approach when crafting our own. Think grown-up lemonade. Fresh lemons and lemon peel pair with cardamom and lemon verbena for a lighter and fresher citrus flavour.

DILLON'S ORANGECELLO

Orangecello is made in the same fashion as limoncello but uses bitter-orange peel with botanicals such as red peppercorns and juniper to give a delicious bitter finish. We enjoy using it in cocktails that call for a bitter liqueur like Campari or Aperol.

CASSIS

This classic French liqueur is made with black currants and sugar. Lovely to sip over ice after a meal, but also the perfect partner to sparkling wine in a Kir Royale (page 202).

DILLON'S CASSIS

Our Cassis is crafted using local black currants. The fresh berries are steeped in our rye-based spirit and sweetened with organic cane sugar. Similar to our limoncello and orangecello, we keep the sugar content lower than most commercially available bottles of cassis to show off the fresh berries.

PEACH SCHNAPPS

North American peach schnapps generally have a lower alcohol percentage and are made with a neutral spirit that has been sweetened and flavoured. Try it in the Mariposa Float (page 123) or add it to your next batch of Sangria (page 103).

For a natural alternative, try our small-batch Peach Schnapps, crafted using fresh Niagara peaches and our grain-to-glass rye spirit, and then lightly sweetened to perfection.

ORANGE LIQUEUR

Orange liqueurs such as Cointreau and triple sec are made using a neutral spirit base and both sweet and bitter oranges, and are sweetened with sugar. They are typically used to make a Margarita (page 60). Grand Marnier is also an orange liqueur, but it starts with a cognac/brandy base to which distilled orange essence and sugar are added; it has a richer, oaky character and a heavier mouthfeel. A good example of a cocktail using Grand Marnier is the Pumpkin Spice Old-Fashioned (page 152).

MARASCHINO LIQUEUR

This liqueur has an intense Marasca cherry aroma and flavour. Luxardo maraschino liqueur is the most commonly available brand. Use it in a Martinez (page 205) or an Aviation (page 225).

ELDERFLOWER LIQUEUR

Crafted using elderflowers, this sweet liqueur gives a well-balanced profile of floral notes to many cocktails. St-Germain is the most widely available brand. Elderflower liqueur can be found in such cocktails as the Elder Orange Fizz (page 198) and the Vespère (page 164).

GREEN OR YELLOW CHARTREUSE

Green Chartreuse is a French liqueur crafted with 130 herbs and botanicals. Yellow Chartreuse is milder and sweeter than its green counterpart.

FRUIT SPIRITS

Fruit spirits are crafted using wine or fruit as their base. The fruit is fermented and then distilled, fewer times than most spirits, to retain as much of the fruit flavour as possible. Fruit spirits are typically made using grapes, pears, apricots, peaches, or other fruits native to the region where the spirit is being produced. They can be aged in casks or kept unoaked.

EAU-DE-VIE

Eaux-de-Vie are unaged fruit spirits that are clear and colourless. They are available from all corners of the world and, like brandy, can be made from whatever local fruit is available. Eaux-de-vie are most often enjoyed after dinner as a digestivo.

BRANDY

Brandy is a fruit spirit that has been aged in oak barrels or casks. It adds great oak character to classic cocktails like the Sidecar (page 210). Brandy is traditionally made from a grape base, but other fruits can be used as well. Examples of brandies include Cognac, Calvados, Applejack, or Pear Brandy.

We produce a small batch of aged Pear Brandy each year using local Bartlett pears that have been pressed, fermented, and then distilled twice in our copper pot still before heading to an oak barrel to age for one to two years. It is aged in first-fill bourbon casks and refinished wine barrels so the oak character is lighter, allowing the clean pear flavour to shine through.

BITTER APERITIVO/DIGESTIVO

Bitter liqueurs crafted with a blend of herbs and botanicals are traditionally enjoyed before dinner as a standalone offering or in cocktails where bitterness is required.

CAMPARI/APEROL

Where a recipe calls for Campari or Aperol, you can safely use the brand that you have on hand. They differ in sweetness and alcohol content, but are an integral part of so many classic cocktails, among them the Aperitivo Spritz (page 124) and Paper Plane (page 175).

AMARO

Italian for "bitter," amaro is an herbal liqueur traditionally served after dinner as a digestivo. Today, it can be found in a number of cocktail recipes, including some of our own, such as the Golden Horseshoe (page 111) and Weekend in Niagara (page 140). Amaro is typically produced by macerating a blend of herbs, roots, flowers, bark, and/or the peels of various citrus fruits in alcohol. The base alcohol is usually a neutral spirit or wine. After distillation, the mixture can be either aged in casks or bottled without aging.

DILLON'S BLACK WALNUT AMARO

Our first batches of amaro have been crafted using fresh black walnuts harvested just down the road from the distillery. The black walnuts, outer husk and all, steep in our rye-based alcohol for anywhere from six months to two years. Then we add them to a vermouth-like wine base to create a bitter yet balanced spirit.

FORTIFIED WINES

Fortified wines are wines that have a spirit added to them—typically a neutral spirit or brandy. Examples of fortified wines in addition to those listed below are sherry, port, and madeira.

VERMOUTH

This aromatic fortified wine is crafted using various herbs, botanicals, roots, flowers, and barks. Two main styles of vermouth are used most commonly: dry vermouth and sweet vermouth. Although they each bring different flavours to a cocktail, both are pillars for a wide number of classic drinks, including the Martini (page 39) and Negroni (page 47, 189).

DILLON'S SWEET VERMOUTH

We began crafting sweet vermouth in 2016 using Niagara wine as the base and fortifying it with our grape spirit that has had botanicals steeped in it. Our recipe of botanicals includes vanilla, wormwood, gentian, strawberries, and citrus. The vermouth is darkened with burnt sugar and sweetened with organic cane sugar.

DRY VERMOUTH

As its name suggests, dry vermouth is dry, containing very little residual sugar. It is light in colour and is the perfect partner to gin in a Classic Martini (page 39). It is more herbaceous than sweet vermouth, with a light to medium body and a cooling sensation on the palate.

LILLET BLANC

Classified as an aromatized wine or wine-based aperitivo, Lillet Blanc is a fortified wine that has been flavoured with herbs, spices, or fruit. It is used in such classic cocktails as the Vespère (page 164) and Corpse Reviver #2 (page 217).

BITTERS

We like to think of bitters as the salt and pepper for your cocktail. Long regarded as one of the most important components of a cocktail, bitters are a concentrated flavour additive made by macerating botanicals (anywhere from five to twenty in each recipe) with fruit and herbs in a strong alcohol. Because they are so intense in flavour, a few dashes are often all that's necessary to give a cocktail a deep aromatic flavour and enhance the overall flavour profile of your drink. Using the suggested bitters in each recipe will take your cocktail to the next level. While we hope that you will use bitters in all of the recipes you make at home, and encourage you to experiment with them, ultimately, they are optional.

CRAFTING THE PERFECT COCKTAIL

When it comes to crafting cocktails, we at Dillon's have always taken the "less is more" approach. Our goal is to use fewer ingredients and allow each of them to shine. Especially when you are at home making drinks, it's important that the cocktails you make are tasty and balanced, but still easy to prepare.

THE FOUR FLAVOUR COMPONENTS

Basic cocktail flavours or components can be broken out into four categories: sweet, sour, bitter, and alcohol. Some cocktails possess all four of the components—think of something like a Paper Plane (page 175). Others have three of the components, like an Old-Fashioned (page 152) or a Negroni (page 47, 189), which incorporate the alcohol, sweet, and bitter components.

When building a drink—whether you're following one of our recipes or creating your own cocktail—you'll need to make sure that you combine at least three of the flavour components, and that they are well balanced. Next time you order a cocktail at a restaurant or bar or make one at home, see if you can pinpoint the flavour components. If you can identify only one of them (maybe you only taste sweetness or bitterness), it's possible the cocktail is not balanced.

Here are a few notes on the main flavour components and ways that you can incorporate each in the drinks you make at home.

SWEET

With most cocktails, the sweet component comes from simple syrup (page 240). Controlling the sweetness of a drink by changing the amount of simple syrup is easy. If a recipe calls to use 1 ounce of syrup but you find it too sweet, or not sweet enough, you can easily make the necessary adjustment. If the imbalance is a result of sweetness that comes from a spirit, like a liqueur, that sweetness level is harder to adjust and you have to make changes to other components of the drink to restore the equilibrium, such as adding more sour (citrus) or bitter (mainly from the addition of bitters) components.

SOUR

Sour flavour comes from citrus in the form of lemon or lime. Grapefruit and orange will also add a sour note to cocktails but not to the same degree that lemon and lime will. This is another of those flavour components that is easy to adjust as needed.

BITTER

Bitterness can be balanced by using a few different ingredients. Adding cocktail bitters is the simplest way to increase bitterness, but you can also use spirits like Campari or Aperol or other bitter aperitivi, which lend a strong bitter-orange taste.

ALCOHOL

Is your drink boozy enough? In a standard 4-ounce cocktail, close to half the liquid should be spirit (between 1½ and 2 ounces). If you can't taste the flavour of the base spirit, you might need to up the spirit content. On the flip side, if *all* you can taste is the alcohol, try adding both a sweet and a sour component until it's just right.

SHAKEN VS. STIRRED

Have you ever wondered when you should shake a cocktail and when you should stir one? Well, it's one of those questions that stirs up some debate.

You will notice that some of the recipes in this book instruct you to shake a cocktail while others suggest that you stir it. There is a general rule that we try to stick to as much as we can—and you can use it too when you're crafting new combinations at home. But, like any rule, there are always exceptions, so feel free to experiment—shake one, stir another, and see which way it turns out better.

WHEN TO SHAKE

Shake cocktails when the recipe includes ingredients such as fruit juices (including citrus), cream liqueurs, simple syrup, sour components, egg white, or dairy. Essentially, use the shaker when you need to ensure that every ingredient is fully integrated into the finished drink's flavour.

Because shaking is intense, it will also break down more ice and add a greater amount of water to the drink. A little bit of dilution is actually a good thing because it results in a more balanced cocktail in which all the ingredients marry together to create one cohesive flavour.

WHEN TO STIR

Stir cocktails that are mainly spirit based. Stirring is a gentler technique for mixing cocktails, though it's often done for at least 20 to 30 seconds, which is longer than the typical shake. It is used to delicately combine the cocktail's ingredients with a perfect amount of dilution from the ice.

ICE

Ice plays a major role in a finished cocktail, so it is something you should take seriously if you want to make high-quality cocktails at home. Ice not only dilutes more spirit-heavy cocktails but also helps to keep drinks cool. With the exception of hot drinks, or those that use champagne, like a French 75 (page 36), ice is used in almost all cocktails. Depending on the cocktail you are crafting, certain types of ice may be more appropriate than others. When preparing a cocktail, the ice should be the last ingredient you add, right before you shake or stir your drink. And when it comes to making ice, following a few simple tips will ensure you have only the finest specimens.

- First, be sure to use good-quality filtered or purified water. These frozen cubes are going to melt into your cocktail and you don't want any impurities to ruin the flavour of the drink.
- Second, you may want to consider aesthetics. To achieve a clear ice cube, use hot water. Studies show that hot water will help to give you the clearest, non-cloudy cubes. Freezing your ice cubes inside a cooler that has been placed in a deep freezer is also said to aid in crystal-clear cubes of ice.
- Finally, do your best to use your ice as soon as possible. If you let ice sit in the freezer for too long, it will start to pick up the flavours of whatever else is in there, which might also spoil a drink.

CRUSHED ICE

Crushed ice melts quickly and adds more water to drinks than ice cubes or blocks do. Usually, it is used when making frozen drinks because cubes can clog your blender's blades. To make crushed ice, put some ice cubes in an ice bag and hit them with a mallet, or toss some ice cubes into a resealable plastic bag and a use a rolling pin to break them down.

ICE CUBES

Ice cubes can be used when making almost any kind of cocktail—whether a drink is shaken, stirred, or served on the rocks. The larger the surface area of an ice cube, the slower it will melt. This means that a drink made with larger ice cubes will be less diluted than one made with smaller ones. If you find that your drinks come out too watery, try using larger cubes.

LARGE BLOCK

Years ago, before so many fancy and elaborate ice moulds and trays were available, all ice used in cocktails was chipped off a large block, typically a few feet in length. Fast-forward, and now large blocks are used mainly for keeping punch cocktails cold when they are served. Large-block moulds in various shapes can be purchased for this purpose. Using large blocks of ice means a slower dilution, which comes in handy if you're pre-batching and serving cocktails at an event in a punch bowl or drink dispenser. You can freeze fruit or edible flowers in these large blocks to increase the overall aesthetic of the presentation.

TOOLS

Having a good set of cocktail tools can make crafting a cocktail easier, but you likely have things in your kitchen at home that will do the trick just as well.

The cocktails in this book don't require too many specialized tools. Most can be found in any cocktail specialty store or in a well-stocked kitchen supply shop. Below is a full list of the tools that are handy to have; we have made recommendations for the ones that are the must-haves.

SHAKERS

COBBLER SHAKER

The shaker most people start out using consists of a large metal mixing tin, a metal lid with a built-in strainer, and a smaller cap to cover the strainer. Using a cobbler shaker is as simple as adding your ingredients, securing the lid, and giving the whole thing a shake. Cobbler shakers don't require any additional tools to mix a drink thanks to the built-in strainer, and it is easy to fit their parts together, making them great for beginners.

BOSTON SHAKER

Simpler than the cobbler shaker in design, though a little bit trickier to use at first, the Boston shaker usually consists of a thick mixing glass and a slightly larger metal tumbler or tin. In some cases, both pieces are metal. To use a Boston shaker, pour the ingredients into the mixing glass, add ice, then place the metal tumbler on top with its open side down. Seal the whole thing shut by giving the bottom of the metal tumbler a firm hit with the palm of your hand. Once you've shaken your drink, the two parts can be separated by hitting the side of the metal tumbler where it meets the mixing glass with the palm of your hand. This can be a tad difficult to get the hang of when you're starting out, but with a bit of practice, breaking the seal between the two pieces soon becomes an easy task. Because the Boston shaker does not have a built-in strainer, you will need a strainer to keep ice and any other solids out of a drink when pouring it into your glass. A Boston shaker is our shaker of choice, but a good at-home alternative is a mason jar with lid. If using a mason jar, you will still need a strainer to keep your cocktails free of any solids.

MIXING GLASS

The rule of thumb is that spirit-forward cocktails are stirred rather than shaken. You can stir a cocktail in a variety of vessels (a shaker or a mason jar, for example), but some of the Japanese-style mixing glasses available today are as beautiful as they are functional. They are sturdy thanks to their thick glass walls and solid, flat bases. Most are large enough to mix two cocktails, and with a built-in pour spout, they make the perfect addition to your home bar. We definitely recommend investing in a good-quality mixing glass. It will add beauty to your bar cart and will last a lifetime.

BAR SPOON

A long-handled spoon is used for stirring cocktails. Some cocktail recipes measure ingredients in bar spoons, and most bar spoons measure 1 teaspoon of liquid. The handle of a bar spoon is usually thin and threaded to make the spoon easier to grip and twirl between your fingers. Many also come with a forked end (trident spoon) to easily spear garnishes. This is a tool you should invest in if you plan to frequently stir cocktails in a mixing glass, but a long kitchen spoon will work in a pinch.

STRAINERS

HAWTHORNE STRAINER

Most often used alongside a Boston shaker, this strainer fits neatly over the mouth of the shaker and is designed so that you can hold it in place with just one or two fingers while pouring your cocktail with the same hand. The spring component of the strainer can be removed and used when doing a dry shake (shaking the cocktail without any ice) for cocktails containing egg whites. If you're going to buy a strainer, this is the one we recommend, as it is the most versatile option.

JULEP STRAINER

Best used when straining a cocktail from a mixing glass. Julep strainers tend to fit a mixing glass better than a Hawthorne strainer because of their design and shape.

FINE-MESH SIEVE

Used to strain the solids out of cocktails that call for muddled ingredients. When a cocktail calls for a double strain, pour the cocktail through a Hawthorne strainer and through a fine-mesh sieve at the same time. If you are using a cobbler shaker to make cocktails that have muddled fruit or herbs in them, you may want to pass the cocktail through a fine-mesh sieve to ensure you don't get any remnants of those ingredients in your finished cocktail. A fine-mesh sieve requires the use of both hands to pour your cocktail, so it may take a few attempts to get the hang of using it.

MUDDLER

This essential bar tool is designed to smash fresh cocktail ingredients to release their flavours. A muddler is used to make some of the most popular cocktails, including a mojito, a Sazerac (page 218), or any cocktail you want to add flavour to using herbs and fruit. Muddlers can be made from a variety of materials, but they are all about the same size and have the same basic design. Most are made from either wood or stainless steel and are the perfect size to reach the bottom of the average mixing glass or cocktail shaker. They can have a flat bottom for muddling, or they may have teeth to help release the flavour of fresh ingredients.

To use a muddler, simply add the desired fresh fruit and herbs to a cocktail shaker or mixing glass and press down firmly on the ingredients with your muddler multiple times until the fruit is broken down and the oils from the herbs have been released.

JIGGER

Used for measuring liquid cocktail ingredients, a jigger is one of the best investments when it comes to cocktail tools. You will use your jigger to measure every single cocktail you make. Many different styles are available, so find one you like and are comfortable using. Some jiggers are heavier than others, some taller and some shorter. Test a few out to see which ones you like best. We suggest choosing one that has multiple markings. Our favourites include measurements up to 2 ounces in ¼-ounce increments.

BOTTLE OPENER/WINE OPENER

A staple for any home bar. Makes opening bottles of store-bought ginger beer or other mixes a breeze.

MALLET AND ICE BAG

Typically sold in a set, these are used to make crushed ice for a julep or many refreshing summer cocktails. The mallet is made of wood and the bag of canvas. The instructions are simple: add the ice to the bag; hit the bag with the mallet; pour the ice into the glass. In a pinch, you can use a sealable plastic bag and meat tenderizer or rolling pin.

COCKTAIL PICKS

Wooden or metal picks are always good to have on hand to help garnish your cocktail. Whether you want to garnish a Manhattan with a cherry or add a cucumber ribbon to your summer sipper, cocktail picks will always come in handy.

CITRUS JUICER/REAMER

A quick and easy way to juice fresh citrus for your cocktail. We are firm believers in always using fresh juice in cocktails. A number of styles are available, but the one we use most often is a simple hand citrus squeezer with handles. An inexpensive wooden hand reamer does the job, too.

POUR SPOUT

Though not a must-have for the home cocktail maker, pour spouts for spirit bottles make prepping drinks much easier and cleaner. We recommend using an ultra-simple metal spout.

TONGS

Small tongs are good to have on hand for ice service or for garnishing cocktails.

FUNNEL

A funnel is useful for transferring homemade syrups and shrubs from pots to sealable bottles or jars.

ZESTER

A zester can help you create citrus garnishes that are smaller and thinner than a full twist or peel. Great to use when garnishing a delicate cocktail like The Brandy 105 (page 229), which is served in a flute glass with a narrow opening.

GRATER/MICROPLANE

Used to put the finishing touches on a cocktail that calls for freshly grated nutmeg or citrus.

PEELER

Use a peeler to help you create beautiful citrus garnishes. Any tried-and-true vegetable peeler will work.

BLENDER

Not just for margaritas, a blender is also used for extracting juice from fresh cocktail ingredients such as cucumbers and strawberries. When using a blender, remember to remove any pits from the fruit, cut the fruit into small cubes, and blend on high speed to ensure that no large chunks of fruit remain. At times, you may need to add a small amount (a few teaspoons to ¼ cup) of water to help the fruit break down. If you have an electric juicer, it can definitely be used in place of a blender.

GLASSWARE

Presenting your cocktails in beautiful glassware can help to elevate even the simplest of drinks. Investing in some quality glasses for your home bar is key. We are big fans of vintage stemware and of eclectic and whimsical glassware in general. You don't need to spend a fortune on glasses, and we love it when people mix and match styles, so be sure to poke around in the next antique shop you visit for some new additions.

Alongside each cocktail recipe in this book, we suggest the type of glass we use when making the cocktail. Our suggestions are just that—suggestions—so feel free to use the glass you have at home or the glass you think would suit the cocktail best.

At the very least, it's nice to have a variety of some of the basic styles of glassware at home to use when entertaining and to truly show off your own personal style in your cocktail creations.

ROCKS

A short tumbler-style glass ideal for drinking spirits on the rocks or for cocktails such as an Old-Fashioned (page 152), Negroni (page 47, 189), or Classic Gin and Tonic (page 35). It is one of the most versatile styles of glassware and can be used for a large number of cocktails. Also known as an old-fashioned glass or a lowball.

HIGHBALL

Great for cocktails served with lots of ice and a straw. Best used with cocktails that have a carbonated component—think Fizz (page 68, 100, 159, 168, 198) or Collins (page 108)—or a Caesar (page 120). Also known as a Collins glass.

SPIRIT TASTER

The ideal stemmed glass for tasting or enjoying spirits neat. With its tulip shape, a spirit taster allows you to smell the most aromatics from spirits, which helps to enhance the flavours once they reach your palate. Perfect for sipping a digestivo like amaro (page 18) after dinner or whisky (page 13) neat.

COUPE

Created in the seventeenth century—before the flute glass—as a vessel to serve champagne in, a coupe is great for cocktails that are shaken and served without ice. It is ideal for such classic cocktails as the Gimlet (page 67), Vespère (page 164), and Classic Martini (page 39) so as not to warm the drink with your hands, though we find ourselves drawn to using coupe glasses for a wide range of cocktails.

FLUTE

Perfect for champagne cocktails like the Kir Royale (page 202) or any drink that includes sparkling wine. The shape of the glass allows for all those pretty bubbles to stay intact.

COPPER MUG

Typically used for a Moscow Mule (page 112). Copper's ability to remain nice and cool gives the cocktail a long-lasting chill.

JULEP CUP

This signature glass was designed specifically to serve a Mint Julep (page 64), which was named the official Kentucky Derby cocktail in 1938. Because it's made of metal (either silver or copper), it will keep your crushed ice cold, though it's best to hold the glass at the bottom and drink with a straw so as not to warm the drink too quickly.

SQUARE WINE GLASS

With a less rounded appearance and a more linear design, this cylindrical glass is an elevated take on a rocks glass. Use a square stemmed vintage wine glass to give your fruit-inspired cocktails like the Squeeze Me Clemmie (page 214) a bit of a classier feel.

MARGARITA

For exactly that: a Margarita (page 60). Its extra-wide opening provides the greatest surface area for a salt/sugar rim, resulting in the perfect ratio of rimmer to cocktail.

ABSINTHE

A few different styles of absinthe glass are available. Some are hand-blown, while others are moulded. Depending on the style of glass, there may be a reservoir in the bottom or a dose line to indicate how much absinthe should be served and how much water should be added. These would be used when preparing a traditional absinthe service (page 201).

SPRING

There is nothing more awakening than the start of warmer weather and longer days. Everything in the garden is waking up from a long winter sleep and buzzing with new life. It's the time to source botanicals and ingredients that are in season, and to brainstorm ideas for new cocktails. Fresh strawberries, rhubarb, and fresh herbs like lavender and thyme are ready to harvest and use in cocktails like The Tea Party (page 52) and the Lavender and Grapefruit Salty Dog (page 55). This is the time for getting inspired to liven up your cocktail lineup with local fruit and herbs.

Our spring-inspired cocktails are clean and crisp, with more gin-based and vodka-based drinks, such as the Cucumber Gimlet (page 67), the Peter Rabbit Punch (page 72), and the Niagara Spring Blossom (page 32). This section's refreshing cocktails are crafted with the most awakening spring days in mind.

COCKTAILS

SNACKS

NIAGARA SPRING BLOSSOM

— MAKES 1 COCKTAIL —

Muddling fresh strawberries in this cocktail gives you the amazing flavour of local fruit and some natural sweetness to balance the earthy characteristics of the anise and crisp notes of the cucumber. In Niagara, where our distillery is located, we typically see the first strawberries popping up at the end of May, so this cocktail is a wonderful way to celebrate the first harvest of an incredible lineup of seasonal fruit.

3 thin unpeeled cucumber slices

3 strawberries, hulled and cut in half

½ ounce fresh lemon juice

1½ ounces gin

2 dashes wormwood bitters or
     anise-flavoured bitters

Handful of ice cubes

1 ounce soda water

Long ribbon of peeled cucumber,
     for garnish

1. Place a coupe glass in the freezer to chill at least 1 hour before you plan to serve the cocktail.

2. In a cocktail shaker, muddle the cucumber with the strawberries and lemon juice.

3. Add the gin, bitters, and ice and shake for 10 to 15 seconds, until the shaker is cold to the touch.

4. Strain the cocktail into the chilled coupe glass, top with the soda water, and garnish with a cucumber ribbon that has been rolled up and speared with a cocktail pick.

Bar Tip: If you have a bottle of Dillon's Strawberry Gin at home, you can replace the strawberries and gin with 1 ounce strawberry gin.

CLASSIC GIN AND TONIC

— MAKES 1 COCKTAIL —

You can never go wrong with a classic G&T, but if you want to have a bit more fun with the age-old drink, take advantage of what is in season by incorporating fresh fruit or herbs (or both!) from the garden (see Bar Tip). If you're not feeling adventurous enough to try crafting the Tonic Syrup (page 243) yourself, you can use store-bought syrup or tonic water instead. There are so many varieties of tonic water to choose from, so have fun testing them out! You'll be surprised by the different flavours they can bring to a cocktail. If you decide to use tonic water instead of Tonic Syrup, omit the soda water from the recipe.

1½ ounces gin

½ ounce Artisan Tonic Syrup
(page 243)

3 or 4 dashes lime bitters

Handful of ice cubes

3 ounces soda water

3 or 4 cucumber slices, for garnish

1. To a rocks glass, add the gin, syrup, and bitters.
2. Add the ice and top with the soda water.
3. Garnish with cucumber slices like we have here or, for a classic gin and tonic, with the citrus wheel of your choice.

Bar Tip: Use one of these great herb and fruit garnish combinations to up your G&T game: a rosemary sprig and an orange slice; raspberries and basil leaves; a lime wheel and a handful of mint leaves.

ROSE GIN FRENCH 75

— MAKES 1 COCKTAIL —

A traditional French 75 is made with dry gin, champagne, lemon juice, and sugar. Since we suggest using a liqueur-style gin for this recipe, you really don't need to add more sweetness in the form of sugar—the Rose Gin adds the perfect amount of sweetness. We think the Rose Gin French 75 is the perfect addition to any Sunday brunch with friends or even as a welcome cocktail for any gathering!

1½ ounces Dillon's Rose Gin

¼ ounce fresh lemon juice

2 dashes pear bitters

Handful of ice cubes

3 ounces dry sparkling wine or
    dry champagne

Lemon twist, for garnish

1. Add the gin, lemon juice, and bitters to a cocktail shaker. Add the ice and shake for 10 to 15 seconds.

2. Strain into a flute glass or a coupe glass and top with the sparkling wine or dry champagne.

3. Using a peeler, peel a strip of lemon zest from a fresh lemon. Cut into a long, thin strip using a knife, then twist the peel around a wooden spoon handle and hold for 20 seconds to achieve a tight curl. Garnish with the lemon twist.

Bar Tip: If you prefer to stick with tradition for your French 75 cocktail, simply replace the Rose Gin with dry gin and add ½ ounce simple syrup (page 240).

CLASSIC MARTINI

— MAKES 1 COCKTAIL —

Everyone loves a classic dry martini. But when it comes to making one, the amount of vermouth that should be used is up for debate. Some simply wave the cap of the vermouth bottle over their glass to leave a subtle aroma behind, while others use an atomizer to add a hint of vermouth to the finished drink. Then there are those who commit more fully by measuring their vermouth in a jigger. In this recipe, we go all in, but you can adjust the amount of vermouth to suit your taste. The same rule applies to whether you use vodka or gin—just go with the spirit you like best. We like to stir our martinis, but we won't be offended if you decide to shake yours à la James Bond.

2½ ounces gin or vodka

½ ounce dry vermouth

1 teaspoon brine from Quick Pickled
    Onions (page 248; optional)

Handful of ice cubes

1 olive or Quick Pickled Onion
    (page 248), for garnish

1. Place a martini glass in the freezer to chill at least 1 hour before you plan to serve the cocktail.

2. Add the gin or vodka, dry vermouth, and brine (if using) to a mixing glass. Add the ice and stir for at least 20 to 30 seconds.

3. Strain the cocktail into the chilled martini glass and garnish with an olive or Quick Pickled Onion on a cocktail pick.

Bar Tip: To give your martini an elegant and classic look when serving, strain it into a coupe glass instead.

LEMONY LEMONADE

— MAKES 8 COCKTAILS —

Since limoncello is one of the most popular spirits sold here at the distillery, it became the inspiration for this drink. The mint's fresh aroma and taste make it a nice addition to the cocktail, both in the lemonade and as a garnish. You can of course steep or add any number of other fresh herbs to the lemonade. Thyme, lemon verbena, vanilla, lavender, or basil can be used to put your own spin on the recipe.

FOR THE LEMONADE
(MAKES ABOUT 3 CUPS)

¾ cup organic cane sugar

¾ cup water

Handful of fresh mint leaves

2½ cups fresh lemon juice
    (about 12 lemons)

FOR THE COCKTAILS

3 cups lemonade

1½ cups vodka

¾ cup limoncello

36 dashes lemon bitters

8 handfuls of ice cubes

12 ounces soda water (optional)

Fresh mint leaves, for garnish

1. Make the lemonade. Combine the sugar and water in a small pot and bring to a boil. Reduce the heat to a simmer, stirring until the sugar has dissolved. Remove the pot from the heat and add the mint leaves. Cover and steep for approximately 15 minutes.

2. Strain the mixture into a glass pitcher with a lid.

3. Add the lemon juice and stir. Store the lemonade in the covered pitcher in the refrigerator until it is time to make the cocktail.

4. Make the cocktail. To a glass pitcher, add the lemonade, vodka, limoncello, and bitters. Stir to mix.

5. When you're ready to serve the cocktails, fill 8 rocks glasses with ice. Divide the cocktail evenly into each glass and top with soda water, if desired. Garnish with mint leaves.

RHUBARB SOUR

·············

— Makes 1 cocktail —

We try as much as possible not to repeat custom cocktails we create for an event, but sometimes one comes along that is so good, we can't help but share it again and again. This cocktail has become one of our springtime favourites. It offers the perfect balance of tart flavour from the rhubarb and lime juice, and natural sweetness from the gin and the candied rhubarb garnish.

FOR THE CANDIED RHUBARB
(MAKES 8 TO 10 PIECES,
ENOUGH FOR 8 COCKTAILS)

·············

2 medium rhubarb stalks

1 cup granulated sugar

FOR THE RHUBARB SYRUP
(MAKES 2 CUPS, ENOUGH
FOR 8 COCKTAILS)

·············

1½ cups chopped rhubarb

1 cup granulated sugar

1 cup water

FOR THE COCKTAIL

·············

2 ounces gin

2 ounces rhubarb syrup

1 ounce fresh lime juice

4 dashes rhubarb bitters

Handful of ice cubes, more for serving

1 ounce soda water

Candied rhubarb, for garnish

1. Prepare the candied rhubarb. Preheat the oven to 440°F and line a baking sheet with parchment paper.

2. Trim the ends off the rhubarb stalks, wash them (but don't dry them), and cut them into finger-length pieces. Pour the sugar onto a small plate. While the rhubarb pieces are still damp, roll them in the sugar, making sure that they are covered evenly. Arrange the sugar-coated rhubarb on the baking sheet, leaving space between each piece. Bake for 1 hour, or until almost all of the liquid from the rhubarb has evaporated and the stalks start to look crisp. Let cool on the baking sheet. The rhubarb pieces can be stored in an airtight container in the refrigerator for up to 2 weeks.

3. Make the rhubarb syrup. Combine the rhubarb, sugar, and water in a medium pot and bring to a boil. Reduce the heat to a simmer, stirring until the sugar has dissolved. Remove the pot from the heat and leave the rhubarb to steep in the liquid for at least 1 hour, pressing the rhubarb occasionally with a wooden spoon to extract additional flavour. Once cooled and steeped, the liquid should have a pink hue to it. Strain the syrup into an airtight container. Stored in the refrigerator, it will keep for up to 2 weeks.

4. Make the cocktail. Add the gin, syrup, lime juice, and bitters to a cocktail shaker. Add the ice and shake for 10 to 15 seconds.

5. Strain the cocktail into a rocks glass or a mason jar filled with fresh ice cubes. Top with soda water and garnish with a piece of the candied rhubarb.

WHISKY SOUR

A whisky sour is a cocktail that showcases the versatility of dark spirits. It is a light and fresh drink that can certainly quench your thirst as the weather starts to get nice and warm. We tend to think of this cocktail as a good transition drink in two very different ways. First, it's the perfect drink to take you from the colder winter months, with their rich whisky-based cocktails, into spring, when cocktails start to brighten up. But it's also a great cocktail to ease the transition if you're new to enjoying aged spirits, thanks to its tart lemon flavour and the sweetness that the syrup brings.

2 ounces rye whisky

1 ounce fresh lemon juice

¾ ounce simple syrup (page 240)

2 dashes aromatic bitters

1 egg white

Handful of ice cubes, more for serving

1 Whisky-Soaked Cherry (page 249)

1. Add the whisky, lemon juice, syrup, bitters, and egg white to a cocktail shaker. Shake vigorously for at least 10 to 15 seconds.

2. Remove the spring portion of a Hawthorne strainer and drop the spring into the shaker. Add the ice and shake vigorously for another 30 seconds. The spring will help to froth up the egg white.

3. Remove the spring and strain the cocktail either into a rocks glass filled with fresh ice cubes or into a coupe glass and keep it neat. Garnish with a Whisky-Soaked Cherry that has been speared with a cocktail pick.

SPRING NEGRONI

— MAKES 1 COCKTAIL —

We love a good Negroni, but with a drink so classic, putting your own spin on it can be a challenge. This recipe swaps out some of the traditional ingredients for ones that are a bit lighter for a fresh take on the classic. To change the flavour profile slightly, feel free to use one of the Dillon's liqueur-style gins—especially the Rose Gin—in place of the gin.

1 ounce gin

1 ounce sweet vermouth

½ ounce Campari or bitter aperitivo
    of choice

½ ounce orangecello or orange liqueur
    of choice

3 dashes ginger bitters

Handful of ice cubes

1 (2-inch-square) ice cube

1 orange peel and dried rose petals
    (optional), for garnish

1. Add the gin, vermouth, Campari, orangecello, and bitters to a mixing glass. Add the ice cubes and stir for 20 to 30 seconds.

2. Place a large fresh ice cube in a rocks glass and strain the cocktail into the glass.

3. Using a peeler, peel a large strip of orange peel from a fresh orange. Rub it around the rim of the glass to release oils. Garnish with the orange peel and sprinkle dried rose petals (if using) on top.

Bar Tip: If you don't have orangecello or orange liqueur at the ready, you can increase the measure of Campari or bitter aperitivo to 1 ounce instead.

AMERICANO

No, we aren't talking about a caffeinated beverage. This is a simple, classic low-alcohol sipper to enjoy, perhaps as a pre-dinner cocktail. It is light and refreshing, but still allows the sweetness from the vermouth to shine through, while the orange peel garnish provides just the right amount of bitterness to finish off the cocktail, leaving a hint of citrus aroma on the nose.

Ice cubes

1 ounce sweet vermouth

1 ounce Campari

½ ounce soda water

Orange peel or orange wedge,
    for garnish

1. Fill a highball glass with ice cubes and add the vermouth and Campari. Top with the soda water and gently stir to combine.
2. Using a peeler, peel a strip of orange peel from a fresh orange, or cut a wedge of orange to garnish the cocktail.

Bar Tip: For an earthy and more nutty variation on this classic, try using ½ ounce Campari and ½ ounce amaro in place of the 1 ounce of Campari.

Perfect Sunday

— MAKES 1 COCKTAIL —

This cocktail is equal parts light, fresh, rich, and spicy. Contributed by Nathan Head, of Vine Arts Wine and Spirits in Calgary, Alberta, it's a great transition cocktail from the chill of winter to bright and blossoming spring. There's a nice amount of spice from the pepper in the syrup, but it's balanced nicely by the rich honey notes. Adding fresh lemon juice brings a subtle kick of acidity and plays well with both styles of gin.

FOR THE BLACK PEPPER HONEY SYRUP (MAKES ¾ CUP, ENOUGH FOR 12 COCKTAILS)

½ cup liquid pure honey

½ cup boiling water

1½ teaspoons freshly cracked black pepper

FOR THE COCKTAIL

1 ounce dry gin

1 ounce Dillon's Cherry Gin or cherry liqueur of choice

½ ounce lemon juice

½ ounce black pepper honey syrup

Handful of ice cubes, more for serving

3 ounces tonic water

1 fresh rosemary sprig, for garnish

1. Make the black pepper honey syrup. Combine the honey, boiling water, and pepper in a mason jar, stir, and let cool with the lid off. Once cooled, strain out the pepper using a fine-mesh sieve. The syrup will keep in an airtight container in the refrigerator for approximately 2 weeks.

2. Make the cocktail. Add the gin, Cherry Gin, lemon juice, and syrup to a cocktail shaker. Add the ice and shake vigorously for 10 to 15 seconds.

3. Strain the cocktail into a highball glass filled with fresh ice cubes. Top with the tonic water and garnish with a sprig of rosemary.

Bar Tip: If you do not have a bottle of Dillon's Cherry Gin at home, try making your own. Pour 25 ounces of your favourite gin into a wide-mouth jar with a tight-fitting lid. Muddle 1 cup of pitted fresh sweet cherries, then add the fruit and all the juices to the gin. Allow the mixture to steep with the lid on for up to 1 week. When you are happy with the amount of cherry flavour, strain out the cherries using a fine-mesh sieve and transfer the infused gin to an airtight container or back to the original bottle for storage. You can add simple syrup (page 240) to taste, or leave it dry. When stored in an airtight container, your cherry gin will last indefinitely.

THE TEA PARTY

The perfect drink for an afternoon tea party or a bridal shower. It's also a great excuse to dust off those family-heirloom teacups and saucers you have on display but never seem to use. The floral notes from the gin, honey, tea, and lemon make one of the best flavour combinations around. This drink is light and fresh, with the perfect amount of sweetness. If you favour tart flavour over sweet, you can always use less of the Honey Syrup (page 241) to allow more of the lemon's acidity to shine through.

3 ounces cold Earl Grey tea

1¼ ounces gin

¾ ounce Honey Syrup (page 241)

½ ounce fresh lemon juice

2 or 3 dashes lemon bitters

2 fresh lavender sprigs, more for garnish

Handful of ice cubes, more for serving

1. Add the tea, gin, syrup, lemon juice, bitters, and lavender sprigs to a cocktail shaker. Add the ice and shake for 10 to 15 seconds.

2. Strain the cocktail into a rocks glass or a tea cup, add fresh ice cubes to fill the glass, and garnish with fresh lavender.

LAVENDER AND GRAPEFRUIT SALTY DOG

— MAKES 8 COCKTAILS —

A refreshing and lively cocktail for a Sunday brunch or a Mother's Day get-together. It is so easy to make that even the busiest host will be able to pull it off in a pinch! Since the recipe doesn't call for any carbonated ingredients that will lose their fizz, you can also make the pitcher of cocktails ahead of time. Lavender and grapefruit may not be a classic flavour combination, but the floral notes from the lavender complement the tart acidity of the grapefruit in a way that is incredibly pleasing.

FOR THE LAVENDER-INFUSED
VODKA (MAKES 25 OUNCES,
ENOUGH FOR 25 COCKTAILS)

1 (25-ounce/750 mL) bottle vodka
1 tablespoon dried lavender flowers

FOR THE COCKTAILS

1 cup coarse sea salt
1 grapefruit wedge
3 cups fresh grapefruit juice
(about 3 grapefruits)
1 cup lavender-infused vodka
24 dashes orange bitters
Crushed ice (page 23)

1. Make the lavender-infused vodka. Using a funnel, add the lavender to the bottle of vodka. Put the lid back on and leave the vodka on your counter or bar to steep for up to 5 days, shaking the mixture a few times each day. Taste test the vodka as you go to see when you are happy with the amount of lavender flavour present in the spirit; we find that 4 or 5 days is the perfect amount of time. When you have achieved enough of the lavender flavour to suit your taste, strain out the lavender using a fine-mesh sieve and return the vodka to its bottle. The infused vodka will keep indefinitely.

2. Rim the glasses. Pour the salt onto a small plate. Wet the rims of 8 rocks glasses using the grapefruit wedge, then turn the outside rim of each glass in the salt.

3. Make the cocktail. Add the grapefruit juice, vodka, and bitters to a pitcher. Stir to combine. Keep in the refrigerator until ready to use.

4. When you're ready to serve the cocktails, fill each rimmed glass three-quarters full with crushed ice. Divide the cocktail evenly among the glasses and serve.

Bar Tip: If you prefer to keep the drink a bit more classic, replace the lavender-infused vodka with plain vodka. If you want to try something more adventurous, try infusing your vodka with a jalapeño, rosemary, or even saffron.

BEE'S KNEES

— MAKES 1 COCKTAIL —

A classic cocktail you can easily transform by infusing the Honey Syrup with fresh herbs or fresh fruit of your choice (see Bar Tip). We've tried this recipe with everything from lavender to basil. The tartness of the fresh lemon juice and the sweetness of the honey syrup ensure that this Prohibition-era drink is perfectly balanced and, as the name suggests, is simply the best!

2 ounces dry gin

1 ounce fresh lemon juice

¾ ounce Honey Syrup (page 241)

3 dashes ginger bitters

Handful of ice cubes

Lemon wheel, for garnish

1. Add the gin, lemon juice, syrup, and bitters to a cocktail shaker. Add the ice and shake for 10 to 15 seconds.

2. Strain the cocktail into a coupe glass and garnish with a lemon wheel.

Bar Tip: If you want to try your hand at an infused honey syrup, add a handful of fresh herbs or 1 cup of fruit when you are heating the mixture in the pot. Let the mixture steep as it cools before straining the solids out with a fine-mesh sieve.

CELERY GIN SOUR

— MAKES 1 COCKTAIL —

Why not pack some veggies into a cocktail when you can? Between the floral aroma of the gin, the crisp, cheek-puckering lemon juice, and the herbaceous notes from the celery, this cocktail will have your taste receptors working overtime. If you want to bring even more of an herbal quality to this tasty beverage, try adding a few dashes of wormwood bitters, either in addition to the ginger bitters or in place of it.

1 ounce gin

1 ounce fresh celery juice (about
    2 stalks, cut into 2-inch pieces;
    see Bar Tip)

1 ounce fresh lemon juice

1 ounce simple syrup (page 240)

4 dashes ginger bitters

Handful of ice cubes, more for serving

Lemon wheel and celery leaves,
    for garnish

1. Add the gin, celery juice, lemon juice, syrup, and bitters to a cocktail shaker. Add the ice and shake for 10 to 15 seconds.
2. Strain the cocktail into a rocks glass filled with fresh ice cubes. Garnish with a lemon wheel and/or celery leaves.

Bar Tip: If you don't have a juicer, purée the celery pieces in a blender until smooth. Pour the purée into a cheesecloth-lined fine-mesh sieve and let the juice drain into a bowl until you have the required amount.

WHITE RYE MARGARITA

— MAKES 8 COCKTAILS —

Here's a great example of a cocktail where we have used Dillon's The White Rye in place of tequila and you would never know the difference. Of course, if you would rather make a more traditional version, toss in your favourite tequila instead! This is a versatile cocktail that you can make in a big batch for an early patio season get-together or to celebrate Cinco de Mayo alongside some fresh Pico de Gallo and Guacamole (page 75).

1 cup coarse sea salt

1 lime wedge

1½ cups Dillon's The White Rye
     or tequila

1 cup Cointreau or orange liqueur
     of choice

1 cup fresh lime juice

½ cup simple syrup (page 240)
     or agave nectar

32 dashes orange bitters

8 handfuls of ice cubes

8 lime wheels, for garnish

1. Rim the glasses. Pour the salt onto a small plate. Wet the rims of 8 margarita glasses using the lime wedge, then turn the outside rim of each glass in the salt. Place the rimmed glasses in the freezer to chill for at least 1 hour before serving.

2. Make the cocktails. Add The White Rye or tequila, Cointreau or orange liqueur, lime juice, syrup, and bitters to a pitcher and stir for 15 to 20 seconds.

3. Add a handful of ice to each rimmed glass and divide the cocktail evenly among them. Garnish each with a lime wheel.

Bar Tip: Modern bartenders have rediscovered the sweet and citrus qualities of oleo-saccharum and use it often. An oleo-saccharum can be made using the fruit or citrus of your choice. Making an oleo-saccharum takes a couple of days, so don't forget to give yourself enough time before you plan on showing off to your pals.

ROYAL VELVET

— Makes 1 cocktail —

This recipe was contributed by Lewis McIver, a young bartending professional based in Toronto, and a Dillon's Cocktail Cup champion who wowed the crowd with his talent. His winning cocktail incorporates an oleo-saccharum, an ingredient commonly used in nineteenth-century bartending to bring an elegant citrus flavour and aroma to cocktails by pulling citrus oil from the rind. We fell in love with this cocktail and its complex flavour—the fresh aroma of the strawberries, the clean and crisp taste of lemon, and the herbal notes from the absinthe.

FOR THE STRAWBERRY OLEO-SACCHARUM (MAKES ABOUT 1 CUP, ENOUGH FOR 10 COCKTAILS)

1 cup lemon peels (about 6 lemons)

1½ cups granulated sugar

2 cups fresh strawberries, hulled and sliced

3 cups simple syrup (page 240)

FOR THE COCKTAIL

1½ ounces dry gin

¾ ounce strawberry oleo-saccharum

¾ ounce fresh lemon juice

½ ounce white port

3 dashes absinthe

Handful of ice cubes, more for serving

1 ounce soda water

½ fresh strawberry and a lemon wheel, for garnish

1. Make the strawberry oleo-saccharum. Place the lemon peels in an airtight container and cover with the sugar. Put the lid on and store at room temperature for 2 days.

2. Meanwhile, place the strawberries in another airtight container and cover with the syrup. Seal the container and store in the freezer for 2 days.

3. Defrost the strawberries. There will be quite a bit of liquid mixed with the syrup.

4. Strain the liquid from both the strawberry and the lemon mixtures through a fine-mesh sieve into an airtight container, pressing both the strawberries and lemon peels with the back of a spoon to extract all the juices and oils. Stir to combine. This is the oleo-saccharum. It can be stored in the refrigerator for up to 1 week.

5. Place a highball glass in the freezer to chill at least 1 hour before you plan to serve the cocktail.

6. Make the cocktail. Add the gin, oleo-saccharum, lemon juice, port, and absinthe to a cocktail shaker. Add the ice and shake for 10 to 15 seconds.

7. Fill the chilled highball glass with fresh ice cubes and strain the cocktail into the glass. Top with the soda water and garnish with half a strawberry and a lemon wheel.

MINT JULEP

Make up a tray of juleps, place your bets, put on a fancy hat, and get ready to watch the ponies. The original mint julep recipe dates back to the early 1800s, but it is best known as the drink of choice for those attending the Kentucky Derby each spring. Traditionally, a mint julep is crafted using bourbon, but here's our take with rye. Using rye whisky will offer a slightly less sweet, spicier taste to the cocktail. Your favourite seasonal fruit would be a great addition to this cocktail. Just add a few pieces to the glass along with the mint, give it all a quick muddle, then proceed with building the cocktail.

5 fresh mint leaves

2 ounces rye whisky

1½ ounces simple syrup (page 240)

Crushed ice (page 23)

Fresh mint sprig, for garnish

1. In either a julep glass or a rocks glass, muddle the mint leaves to release the herb's oils.

2. Add the rye whisky and syrup to the glass. Add crushed ice until it mounds over the top and garnish with a mint sprig.

CUCUMBER GIMLET

This is one of those cocktails that is so crisp and refreshing, you might lose count of just how many you've enjoyed! It comes out a beautiful, vibrant green colour, and the fresh, earthy notes from the cucumber are well balanced by the citrus kick from the lime juice and bitters. This would be the perfect cocktail to enjoy alongside our Warm Potato Salad with DSB Vinaigrette (page 79).

4 fresh mint leaves, more for garnish

1½ ounces gin

1½ ounces fresh cucumber juice
    (about ¼ unpeeled cucumber;
    see Bar Tip)

¾ ounce fresh lime juice

½ ounce simple syrup (page 240)

3 dashes ginger bitters

3 dashes lime bitters

Handful of ice cubes

Cucumber slice, for garnish

1. Place the mint leaves in a cocktail shaker. Add the gin and muddle.

2. Add the cucumber juice, lime juice, syrup, ginger bitters, lime bitters, and ice. Shake for 10 to 15 seconds.

3. Strain the cocktail into a coupe glass and garnish with a cucumber slice and mint.

Bar Tip: 1. If you don't have a juicer, purée the cucumber in a blender until smooth. Pour the purée into a cheesecloth-lined fine-mesh sieve and let the juice drain into a bowl until you have the required amount. 2. Keep the skin on the cucumber to give the drink extra-vibrant colour. One English cucumber will yield approximately ½ cup juice.

RHUBARB AND FENNEL FIZZ

— MAKES 1 COCKTAIL —

If you love the flavour of fennel, then this is the cocktail for you. The combination of vermouth and lemon, and fennel and gin, makes for an exciting mix of flavours thanks to the herbal and vanilla notes from the vermouth, the acidity from the lemon juice, and the rich, almost licorice-like aroma and taste of the fennel.

FOR THE RHUBARB FENNEL SYRUP (MAKES ABOUT 1 CUP, ENOUGH FOR 16 COCKTAILS)

¾ cup finely chopped rhubarb

¾ cup chopped fennel

½ cup granulated sugar

½ cup water

¼ teaspoon orange zest

FOR THE COCKTAIL

1½ ounces sweet vermouth

½ ounce dry gin

½ ounce fresh lemon juice

½ ounce rhubarb fennel syrup

2 dashes wormwood bitters (optional)

Pinch of salt

Handful of ice cubes, more for serving

1 ounce soda water

Rhubarb ribbon and fennel frond, for garnish

1. Make the rhubarb fennel syrup. Combine the rhubarb, fennel, sugar, water, and orange zest in a medium pot. Cook over medium-high heat, stirring occasionally, until the syrup begins to boil and the rhubarb and fennel start to soften and break down, about 5 minutes. Remove the pot from the heat and let cool for 30 minutes.

2. Strain the liquid through a fine-mesh sieve into an airtight container, pushing on the rhubarb and fennel with the back of a spoon to extract any remaining liquid from the pulp. The syrup will keep in the refrigerator for up to 2 weeks.

3. Make the cocktail. Add the vermouth, gin, lemon juice, syrup, bitters (if using), and salt to a cocktail shaker. Add the ice and shake for 10 to 15 seconds.

4. Strain the cocktail into a coupe or stemmed wine glass filled with fresh ice cubes and top with the soda water.

5. Using a peeler, peel a long ribbon of rhubarb. Garnish the cocktail with the rhubarb ribbon and a fennel frond.

ROSEHIP AND HIBISCUS TEA

The amazing pink colour of this cocktail is perfect for spring. For this drink we use a rosehip and hibiscus tea to achieve the cocktail's wonderful colour and floral aromas, but you can use any type of herbal tea and get an equally wonderful drink, just with a different flavour and colour profile. Ginger bitters add extra depth of flavour, but they are optional. A fresh citrus-based bitters would work nicely here as well.

3 ounces brewed rosehip and hibiscus
　　tea

1½ ounces dry gin

½ ounce fresh lemon juice

½ ounce simple syrup (page 240)

2 dashes ginger bitters

Handful of ice cubes, more for serving

Dried rose petals or tea leaves,
　　for garnish

1. Let the tea cool to room temperature. Place the tea in an airtight container and refrigerate until chilled.

2. Add the cold tea, gin, lemon juice, syrup, and bitters to a cocktail shaker. Add the ice and shake for 10 to 15 seconds.

3. Strain the cocktail into a rocks glass filled with fresh ice. Garnish with a sprinkling of dried rose petals or tea leaves.

PETER RABBIT PUNCH

....

— MAKES 8 COCKTAILS —

The inspiration for this punch comes from the fresh-pressed-juice movement that's taking over the world. We hoped to craft a cocktail that was not just delicious and fun, but that packed in a lot of fruits and veggies too. This punch offers the right amount of sweetness thanks to the pineapple juice, with balanced acidity from the lemon juice and Ginger Beer. It not only tastes great, but serving it in a punch bowl with floating fruit and flowers makes for a show-stopping presentation.

1¼ cups fresh pineapple juice (about 1 pineapple, peeled and cored; see Bar Tip)

1 cup store-bought pure carrot juice

½ cup fresh lemon juice

1 cup dry gin

12 dashes ginger bitters

4 to 6 (2-inch-square) ice cubes, for the punch bowl

¾ cup Ginger Beer (page 246; see Bar Tip)

Garnishes: handful of edible flowers, pineapple rings, and lemon slices

Ice cubes, for serving

1. Add the pineapple juice, carrot juice, lemon juice, gin, and bitters to a punch bowl or large glass drink dispenser with a spigot. Stir to combine.

2. Add the large ice cubes and top with the Ginger Beer. Garnish by floating the edible flowers and fruit on top.

3. Alongside the bowl, set out 8 square wine glasses and an ice bucket filled with fresh ice cubes so that guests can add fresh ice to their glasses, if desired.

Bar Tip: 1. If you don't have a juicer, cut the pineapple into 2-inch cubes and add them to a blender. Purée until smooth. Pour the purée into a cheesecloth-lined fine-mesh sieve and let the juice drain into a bowl until you have the required amount. 2. If you don't have a batch of your own homemade Ginger Beer on hand, and don't have time to make some, any non-alcoholic ginger beer from the market will do the trick here—so no pressure.

PICO DE GALLO AND GUACAMOLE

— SERVES 8 TO 10 —

We are huge fans of Cinco de Mayo at the distillery—so much so that we have a party to celebrate each spring. Since we have given you our recipe for a White Rye Margarita (page 60), we felt it appropriate to share some easy-to-craft snacks to go along with your pitcher of chilled cocktails. The pico de gallo and guacamole would also be delicious alongside a crisp and clean Classic Gin and Tonic (page 35) or even an Americano (page 48).

FOR THE PICO DE GALLO

5 garlic cloves, minced

2 jalapeño peppers, seeded and minced

4 cups finely chopped tomatoes (about 6 medium tomatoes)

1½ cups finely chopped onion

1½ cups fresh cilantro, chopped

3 tablespoons lime juice (1 to 2 limes)

1 teaspoon sea salt

½ teaspoon lime zest

3 dashes hot pepper bitters (optional)

FOR THE GUACAMOLE

3 ripe avocados

2 tablespoons finely chopped red onion

1 Roma tomato, diced

1 tablespoon fresh lime juice (about ½ lime)

3 garlic cloves, minced

½ teaspoon sea salt, or to taste

1½ teaspoons finely chopped fresh cilantro

3 to 5 dashes lime bitters (optional)

FOR SERVING

Corn chips

1. Make the pico de gallo. To a medium bowl add the garlic, jalapeños, tomatoes, onion, cilantro, and lime juice. Stir to combine.

2. Cover the bowl with plastic wrap and place it in the refrigerator overnight to allow the flavours to come together. (The flavours will start to improve even if you only have time to let it rest in the refrigerator for a few hours.)

3. Before serving, season with salt, lime zest, and bitters, if desired.

4. Make the guacamole. Cut the avocados in half lengthwise. Remove the pit from each and, using a spoon, scoop the flesh into a medium bowl. Using a fork, mash the avocado to your desired texture—chunky or smooth, the choice is yours.

5. Add the onion, tomato, lime juice, garlic, salt, cilantro, and bitters (if using), and gently fold until well incorporated.

6. Transfer the guacamole to a serving bowl and serve with corn chips alongside the pico de gallo—or do what we do and serve straight from a wood cutting board for a more rustic display.

SPRING PEA CROSTINI

— MAKES 24 CROSTINI —

Fresh, sweet snap peas are a treat to enjoy in the spring—as the main feature of a recipe like this one or as an additional flavour in a garden salad or a warm rice dish. We couldn't decide on just one topping for these crostini bites, so we're sharing a few of the ones we love the most. Enjoy them alongside a Niagara Spring Blossom (page 32) or a refreshing Cucumber Gimlet (page 67), or any other spring cocktail!

1½ cups shelled fresh snap peas

½ cup freshly grated Parmesan cheese

1 medium garlic clove

⅓ cup extra-virgin olive oil,
    more for crostini

Sea salt

Freshly ground black pepper

1 baguette, cut into ½-inch-thick slices,
    for serving

TOPPINGS (OPTIONAL)

Radishes, thinly sliced

Cherry tomatoes, thinly sliced

Strawberries, thinly sliced

Fresh herbs (dill, cilantro, basil),
    chopped

1. Preheat the oven to 350°F.

2. Add the peas, Parmesan, and garlic to the bowl of a food processor. While slowly adding the olive oil, process until the mixture reaches a semi-smooth consistency. Season with salt and pepper to taste.

3. Arrange the baguette slices on a baking sheet. Brush with olive oil on both sides. Lightly season the tops with salt and pepper. Toast the bread until golden and crisp, 12 to 14 minutes, turning halfway through. Let cool to room temperature.

4. Top the toasted baguette slices with the pea mixture and your desired toppings. Serve immediately.

Kitchen Tip: 1. If fresh peas aren't available, you can use thawed frozen peas. 2. For topping combinations, we like radishes with dill, cherry tomatoes topped with cilantro, and sliced strawberries with basil. Feel free to be creative and make your own mouth-watering combinations!

WARM POTATO SALAD WITH DSB VINAIGRETTE

— SERVES 10 —

Bitters of course are not only great in cocktails but also make wonderful additions to dressings, marinades, and even desserts. Here is a great way to incorporate a more traditional, aromatic bitters into a vinaigrette that you can use right away, store in the refrigerator, or package up neatly to use as gifts. For the perfect spring cocktail party hand-held snack, serve this salad in shallow 8-ounce wide-mouth mason jars. Perfect with a Celery Gin Sour (page 59) or Spring Negroni (page 47).

FOR THE DSB VINAIGRETTE

1½ teaspoons minced lemon peel

1 teaspoon granulated sugar

1 teaspoon celery seeds

Salt and pepper

¼ cup white wine vinegar

3 tablespoons fresh lemon juice

1 teaspoon grainy mustard

5 dashes aromatic bitters

⅓ cup extra-virgin olive oil

FOR THE POTATO SALAD

3 pounds multicoloured baby potatoes

1 teaspoon sea salt

1 pound asparagus, trimmed

8 radishes, thinly sliced

½ cup DSB vinaigrette

¼ cup fresh dill, chopped

1. Make the DSB vinaigrette. Combine the lemon peel, sugar, and celery seeds in a small bowl. Season with salt and pepper. Using the back of a spoon, mash together until well combined.

2. Stir in the vinegar, lemon juice, mustard, and bitters. Whisking constantly, slowly drizzle in the olive oil until it is completely incorporated. Adjust seasoning with salt and pepper as needed.

3. Make the potato salad. Add the potatoes to a large pot and add enough water to cover them completely. Add the salt. Bring to a boil over high heat and cook the potatoes for 15 to 20 minutes, or until they are tender when poked with a fork. Drain the potatoes.

4. Meanwhile, bring a second pot of water to a boil over high heat. Add the asparagus and cook for 3 to 5 minutes or until tender. Drain.

5. When both the potatoes and the asparagus are just cool enough to handle, cut each into bite-size pieces. Combine the potatoes, asparagus, and radishes in a large bowl. Drizzle with the vinaigrette and toss to coat. Stir in the chopped dill and serve warm.

CELERY ROOT AND HALIBUT TACOS

— SERVES 10 TO 12 —

Chef Kyle Paton, chef-owner of the Black Lodge in Beamsville, Ontario, is known around the world for his avant-garde cooking techniques and presentation, but when he's at home with his family, he likes to keep it simple. These tacos are great to make on a lazy Sunday afternoon, when you have a bit of time to spend in the kitchen—they are sure to bring the whole gang to the table. If you cannot find ramps at your local farmer's market, use a bunch of green onions instead. Try these tacos along with a batch of Peter Rabbit Punch (page 72) or Lemony Lemonade (page 40).

FOR THE RAMP AND HABANERO SAUCE

1 bunch ramps

1 habanero pepper

2 tablespoons vegetable oil, divided

4 dashes lime bitters

FOR THE TACO SHELLS AND FILLING

2 large celery root bulbs

1 tablespoon sunflower oil

1 cup 2% milk

Sea salt

8 ounces skinless halibut fillet

½ cup vegetable oil

2 tablespoons fresh lemon juice

Lime wedges, for garnish

1. Make the ramp and habanero sauce. Preheat the oven to 450°F and line a baking sheet with parchment paper.

2. Lightly coat the ramps and the habanero pepper with 1 tablespoon of the vegetable oil. Arrange them in a single layer on the baking sheet and bake until they start to char and the leaves of the ramps are nice and dark, 12 to 18 minutes.

3. Transfer the pepper and the ramps to a blender. Add the bitters, and blend until the sauce is thick, adding as much of the remaining tablespoon of vegetable oil as needed. Set aside.

4. Reduce the oven temperature to 350°F.

5. Make the taco shells. Using a vegetable peeler, peel one celery root bulb. Cut it in half. Using a mandoline or a knife, and working from the larger cut side, slice the bulb into rounds the width and thickness of a tortilla. You should wind up with 10 to 12 slices. These will be your tortillas.

6. Heat the sunflower oil in a large cast-iron pan over medium-high heat. Sear the celery root slices for 2 minutes on each side. Stack the celery root tortillas on a plate and cover them with a kitchen towel until it is time to assemble the tacos. Set aside the pan.

7. Make the filling. Peel the remaining celery root bulb and cut it into ½-inch chunks or cubes.

8. In a medium pot, combine the celery root cubes and the milk. Poach the celery root over medium-low heat until tender, 12 to 15 minutes. Drain the remaining milk and season with salt to taste.

9. While the celery root is cooking, cut the halibut into ½-inch pieces. In the cast-iron pan, gently heat the vegetable oil to 130°F. Place the halibut in the oil and cook for 10 minutes, or until the desired texture is achieved. Transfer the fish to a plate. Sprinkle the lemon juice over the fish and season with salt to taste.

10. Assemble the tacos. On a parchment-lined baking sheet, place the tortillas in a single layer and reheat in the oven for 5 minutes. Gently mix the celery root and halibut cubes together and divide them among the celery root tortillas. Pour the ramp and habanero sauce on top, to taste. Finish with a squeeze of lime juice and serve immediately.

SUMMER

The summer months are the busiest time of year for both our distilling and our hospitality teams, which of course means lots of cocktails and lots of visitors to the distillery. Tours of the distillery and garden run daily, and the influx in guests gives the whole space a lively, energized feel. Within a ten-minute drive from the distillery you will find freshly picked peaches, apricots, raspberries, blueberries, watermelons, and plums—not to mention a bounty of fresh herbs for cocktail garnishes and syrups. Similarly, our garden is overflowing with ingredients to harvest, among them cucumbers, black currants, saskatoon berries, and loads and loads of fresh herbs like lemon balm, basil, stevia, and more. The clean and fresh flavours of seasonal fruits and fresh herbs make for some of the most fun and refreshing drinks, like our Strawberry Fields (page 88), Apricot Fizz (page 100), and Watermelon Collins (page 108).

COCKTAILS

SNACKS

WATERMELON MINT AGUA FRESCA

— MAKES 1 COCKTAIL —

Sometimes you come across one of those drinks that can be a little too easy to enjoy. You know what we mean: you are basking in the sun with friends on a beautiful summer afternoon and before you know it, you've all imbibed a few more refreshing bevvies than you thought you had. This ultimate summer party cocktail is always a big hit. The combination of the fresh watermelon and mint with a kick of lime juice makes for a dangerously good drink. Don't say we didn't warn you!

FOR THE WATERMELON AGUA FRESCA

2 (½-inch-thick) watermelon wedges

4 to 6 fresh mint leaves

FOR THE COCKTAIL

1½ ounces watermelon agua fresca

1 ounce vodka

1 ounce simple syrup (page 240)

½ ounce fresh lime juice

6 dashes lime bitters

Handful of ice cubes, more for serving

Fresh mint sprig and a long, thin
    watermelon wedge, for garnish

1. Make the watermelon agua fresca. Cut away and discard the rind from the watermelon, then cut the flesh into 2-inch pieces. Add the watermelon and mint to a blender and purée until smooth. Pour the purée into a cheesecloth-lined fine-mesh sieve and let the juice drain into a bowl until you have the required amount. If you have a juicer, run the watermelon and mint through it instead.

2. Make the cocktail. Add the agua fresca, vodka, syrup, lime juice, and bitters to a cocktail shaker. Add the ice and shake for 10 to 15 seconds.

3. Add fresh ice cubes to a mason jar or a highball glass and strain the cocktail into the glass. Garnish with mint and the watermelon wedge.

Bar Tip: Play around with different fruit and herb combinations in your agua fresca—the possibilities are endless! Or enjoy the agua fresca as a refreshing drink on its own. In general, agua fresca is made with puréed fruit, water (if necessary), a touch of sugar (optional, depending on the sweetness of the fruit), and some lime juice or herbs, if desired. Straining the juice is a personal preference—in some cases we don't even strain out the pulp.

BERRY BRAMBLE

Sometimes a cocktail can transport you to another time and place, and this berry-rich bramble does just that. It takes us back to the days of picking fresh strawberries and eating just as many as what ended up in our basket! This drink is bursting with juicy berry flavours. We use fresh strawberries and blackberries in this recipe, but any combination of fresh berries will work. And if you don't have fresh fruit readily available, give frozen ones a try. Using vodka in this cocktail allows the fresh flavours from the fruit to be the star, but this recipe also works well with gin.

3 strawberries, hulled

3 blackberries

¼ cup water

2 ounces vodka

1 ounce fresh lemon juice

½ ounce simple syrup (page 240)

2 dashes aromatic bitters

Handful of ice cubes

Crushed ice (page 23)

1 ounce soda water (optional)

2 strawberries and 2 blackberries,
    for garnish

1. In a blender, combine the strawberries, blackberries, and water. Blend until smooth. Strain the purée through a fine-mesh sieve into a cocktail shaker.

2. Add the vodka, lemon juice, syrup, and bitters. Add the ice and shake for 10 to 15 seconds.

3. Strain the cocktail into a rocks glass filled with crushed ice. Top with soda water (if using) and garnish with strawberries and blackberries.

Bar Tip: If you wish to make this cocktail in a hurry, you can muddle the fresh fruit in the cocktail shaker instead of puréeing it in a blender. Either strain the fruit out or leave it in if you prefer a cocktail with more texture and mouthfeel.

STRAWBERRY FIELDS

— MAKES 1 COCKTAIL —

Strawberries are by far one of our favourite summer fruits, so as soon as they are in season, we dive right into anything and everything strawberry. This recipe is one of the best ways to show off these sweet, juicy, full-of-flavour berries. We recommend a lavender syrup for this cocktail, but mint or basil syrup would also be a great option. If you opt for one of these alternatives, simply replace the fresh lavender with ½ cup fresh mint or basil when making the syrup.

FOR THE LAVENDER SYRUP
(MAKES 1¾ CUPS, ENOUGH
FOR 18 COCKTAILS)
....

1 cup water
1 cup granulated sugar
4 fresh lavender sprigs

FOR THE STRAWBERRY PURÉE
(MAKES 2 CUPS, ENOUGH FOR
5 COCKTAILS)
....

15 to 20 medium strawberries, hulled
¼ cup water

FOR THE COCKTAIL
....

3 ounces strawberry purée
1½ ounces vodka
¾ ounce lavender syrup
4 dashes lemon bitters
Handful of ice cubes
Fresh lavender sprig, for garnish

1. Make the lavender syrup. Combine the water, sugar, and lavender in a small pot and bring to a boil. Reduce the heat to a simmer, stirring until the sugar has dissolved. Remove the pot from the heat and let cool for 30 minutes. Strain the syrup into an airtight container and store in the refrigerator for up to 2 weeks.

2. Make the strawberry purée. In a blender, combine the strawberries and water. Blend until smooth. The purée will keep in an airtight container in the refrigerator for up to 3 days.

3. Place a rocks glass or a margarita glass in the freezer to chill at least 1 hour before you plan to serve the cocktail.

4. Make the cocktail. Add the strawberry purée, vodka, syrup, and bitters to a cocktail shaker. Add the ice cubes and shake for 10 to 15 seconds.

5. Strain the cocktail into the chilled glass and garnish with a sprig of lavender.

Raspberry Thyme Smash

— Makes 1 cocktail —

Cocktails like this make us dream of warm, sunny summer days. The mix of fresh and bright flavours from the muddled berries and thyme, with the addition of orange liqueur, lime juice, and of course the vodka, makes this one of those summer drinks you'll be serving on repeat. If there's other fresh fruit you prefer, replace the raspberries with something else. Blackberries or strawberries would both be good choices.

2 fresh thyme sprigs, more for garnish

6 raspberries, more for garnish

2 ounces vodka

1 ounce fresh lime juice

1 ounce orangecello or orange liqueur
of choice

½ ounce simple syrup (page 240;
optional)

Handful of ice cubes, more for serving

1 ounce soda water (optional)

1. Remove the leaves from the thyme sprigs and add them to a cocktail shaker. Add the raspberries and muddle. Add the vodka, lime juice, orangecello or orange liqueur, and syrup, if desired. Add the ice and shake for 10 to 15 seconds.

2. Strain the cocktail into a rocks glass filled with fresh ice cubes and top with soda water, if desired. Garnish with raspberries and a sprig of thyme.

PEACHY GREYHOUND

— MAKES 1 COCKTAIL —

A classic Greyhound is made with grapefruit juice, but here we swap it out for fresh peach juice and a splash of bitter liqueur to bring some depth of character to the classic. Peaches are a quintessential summer fruit that we can't get enough of. There is something exciting and satisfying when you find and bite into a perfectly ripe and juicy peach, and we wanted to convey that feeling in this cocktail.

1 tablespoon granulated sugar

Lime wedge

4 ounces fresh peach juice
(about 2 peaches; see Bar Tip)

1½ ounces gin

¼ ounce Aperol

4 dashes lime bitters

Handful of ice cubes, more for serving

Lime wheel and peach slice, for garnish

1. Rim the glass. Pour the sugar onto a small plate. Wet the rim of a rocks glass using the lime wedge, then turn the outside rim of the glass in the sugar.
2. Make the cocktail. Add the peach juice, gin, Aperol, and bitters to a cocktail shaker. Add the ice and shake for 10 to 15 seconds.
3. Fill the rimmed glass with fresh ice, then strain the cocktail into it. Garnish with a lime wheel and a peach slice.

Bar Tip: If you don't have a juicer, remove the pits from the peaches and cut each peach into quarters. Add them to a blender and purée until smooth. Pour the purée into a cheesecloth-lined fine-mesh sieve and let the juice drain into a bowl until you have the required amount.

BEET YA TO IT

·················

— MAKES 1 COCKTAIL —

Here's an unexpected surprise. You don't see something as earthy as a beet used in cocktails too often. This drink has all the earthy tones you would expect from a beet, but its lightness and freshness prevail, making it just right for a late-summer patio gathering with friends. A nice variation would be to use basil in place of the mint to bring in complementary sweet and peppery notes.

FOR THE BEET SYRUP
(MAKES 1½ CUPS, ENOUGH
FOR 8 COCKTAILS)
·············

1 medium red or striped beet, unpeeled
    and chopped
½ cup organic cane sugar
1 cup water

FOR THE COCKTAIL
·············

2 ounces vodka
1½ ounces beet syrup
1 ounce fresh lemon juice
1 dash ginger bitters
1 dash wormwood bitters
Handful of fresh mint leaves,
    more for garnish
Handful of ice cubes
1 ounce soda water (optional)
1 beet chip, for garnish

1. Make the beet syrup. Combine the beet, sugar, and water in a small pot and bring to a boil, stirring to help the sugar dissolve. Let the liquid boil for a minute or two after the sugar dissolves, then remove the pot from the heat and let cool for at least 30 minutes. Strain the syrup into an airtight container. The syrup will keep in the refrigerator for up to 2 weeks.

2. Make the cocktail. Add the vodka, syrup, lemon juice, ginger bitters and wormwood bitters, and mint to a cocktail shaker. Add the ice and shake for 10 to 15 seconds.

3. Strain the cocktail into a coupe glass and top with soda water, if desired. Garnish with the beet chip and mint leaves.

CHERRY SLING

We are lucky to have one of the biggest and best cherry farms just down the road from the distillery in Vineland, Ontario. With both sweet and sour cherries available, we opted to go with the sour ones for this cocktail. The tart flavour from the fresh cherries holds up nicely against the orange liqueur and fresh lime juice, making this a nicely balanced cocktail for all to enjoy.

FOR THE SOUR CHERRY SYRUP
(MAKES ABOUT 2½ CUPS,
ENOUGH FOR 24 COCKTAILS)
....

1 pound sour cherries, stemmed
    and pitted
¾ cup granulated sugar
1 cup water
1 teaspoon lemon zest (about ½ lemon)
2 teaspoons orange zest (about
    ½ orange)

FOR THE COCKTAILS
....

1½ cups dry gin
½ cup Cointreau, or orange liqueur
    of choice
⅔ cup sour cherry syrup
½ cup fresh lime juice (about 6 limes)
7 dashes aromatic bitters
8 handfuls of ice cubes
8 ounces soda water
    (1 ounce per cocktail)
8 lime wheels, for garnish

1. Make the sour cherry syrup. Combine the cherries, sugar, water, lemon zest, and orange zest in a large pot, and bring to a boil. Reduce the heat to low, cover, and simmer for 10 to 15 minutes, until the cherries have fully broken down. Remove the pot from the heat and let cool for at least 30 minutes.

2. Pass the mixture through a fine-mesh sieve, pressing on the solids to extract as much of the liquid as possible. You should finish with roughly 2½ cups of syrup. The syrup will keep in a sealed container in the refrigerator for up to 2 weeks.

3. Make the cocktail. Add the gin, Cointreau, syrup, lime juice, and bitters to a pitcher. Stir until fully mixed.

4. Add 1 handful of ice to each of 8 highball glasses and divide the cocktail evenly among them. Top each glass with 1 ounce soda water. Garnish with a lime wheel.

Bar Tip: If you don't feel inclined to make the syrup, you can replace the gin and sour cherry syrup with about 2 cups Dillon's Cherry Gin Liqueur.

ELECTRIC CURRANT

— MAKES 1 COCKTAIL —

This recipe requires you to make a bottle of currant-infused gin using fresh red currants, but you can use black currants if they are more readily available. Using red currants will result in a slightly more tart drink, whereas black currants are sweeter. Both are great options but we love the vibrant colour the red currants impart. Since a standard spirit bottle holds enough spirit for 25 cocktails, infusing a whole bottle with currants means you either bring the remaining infused gin out for your next gathering, or enjoy it on your own at a slower pace. See the Bar Tip for the ratio of currant to gin to use if you don't want to commit to infusing a full bottle of gin right away.

FOR THE CURRANT-INFUSED
GIN (MAKES 25 OUNCES,
ENOUGH FOR 25 COCKTAILS)
....

1 (25-ounce/750 mL) bottle dry gin

1 cup fresh red currants

FOR THE COCKTAIL
....

1 ounce currant-infused gin

½ ounce fresh lime juice

½ ounce simple syrup (page 240)

3 dashes orange bitters

Handful of ice cubes, more for serving

1½ ounces Ginger Beer (page 246;
    see Bar Tip)

Fresh red currants, for garnish

1. Make the currant-infused gin. Pour the gin into a large jar. Add the currants. Using the back of a spoon, gently press the fruit to break it up slightly. Secure the lid on the jar and let the fruit and gin steep at room temperature for 2 to 3 days.

2. Strain the gin through a fine-mesh sieve into a second airtight jar, pressing the fruit with the back of a spoon to extract as much of the infused spirit as possible. Screw the lid on the jar and store at room temperature. There is no expiration date on the infused gin, so drink it at your leisure.

3. Make the cocktail. Add the gin, lime juice, syrup, and bitters to a cocktail shaker. Add the ice and shake for 10 to 15 seconds.

4. Strain the cocktail into a rocks glass filled with fresh ice cubes. Top with Ginger Beer and garnish with red currants.

Bar Tip: 1. To make a smaller batch of the infused gin, use 2 teaspoons of currants to every 1 ounce of gin. Steep as described above in an airtight container, for the same amount of time. 2. If you don't have a batch of your own homemade Ginger Beer on hand, and don't have time to make some, any non-alcoholic ginger beer from the market will do the trick here—so no pressure.

APRICOT FIZZ

This cocktail reminds us of apricot jam, and boy, do we love apricot jam. This drink is juicy, sweet, and comforting, like a slice of warm fresh bread topped with the classic preserve. To ensure you get the best sweet and aromatic flavour from the fruit, you'll want to use apricots that are really ripe and soft.

2 ounces fresh apricot purée
(about 5 very ripe apricots
peeled, pitted, and sliced)

1½ ounces vodka

¼ ounce fresh lemon juice

3 dashes lemon bitters

Handful of ice cubes, more for serving

2 to 3 ounces soda water

Fresh mint leaf and an apricot slice,
for garnish

1. In a blender, purée the apricots with a splash of water until smooth.

2. Add the purée, vodka, lemon juice, and bitters to a cocktail shaker. Add the ice and shake for 10 to 15 seconds.

3. Strain the cocktail into a highball glass filled with fresh ice cubes. Top with soda water and garnish with the mint and an apricot slice speared on a cocktail pick.

Bar Tip: If you find yourself craving an Apricot Fizz when apricots aren't in season, use 2 ounces apricot jam in place of the fresh purée.

SUMMER SANGRIA

— MAKES 8 COCKTAILS —

Who doesn't love a good ol' batch of sangria? If you have a glass of sangria in your hand, it probably means you're relaxing on a patio somewhere, enjoying the sun and some good company. This recipe combines a few of our favourite things: rosé wine, fresh fruit, and peach schnapps. When picking your rosé for this cocktail, keep in mind that a dry rosé will work better than an off-dry one. If your favourite rosé tends to the sweeter side of the spectrum, scale back the amount of simple syrup so that you still come out with a well-balanced drink.

1 (25-ounce/750 mL) bottle dry rosé

1 cup fresh peach juice (about
    6 peaches; see Bar Tip)

½ cup peach schnapps

⅓ cup simple syrup (page 240)

2 cups sliced peaches (about 3 peaches)

1 cup sliced strawberries (or ½ cup
    sliced strawberries and ½ cup
    whole raspberries)

Ice cubes, for serving

1. Place 8 rocks glasses in the freezer to chill at least 1 hour before you plan to serve the sangria.

2. Add the wine, peach juice, schnapps, and syrup to a large pitcher. Stir well. If desired, add more simple syrup to taste.

3. Add the sliced peaches and strawberries and refrigerate for several hours.

4. Serve the sangria in the chilled rocks glasses with fresh ice.

Bar Tip: If you don't have a juicer, remove the pits from the peaches and cut each peach into quarters. Add them to a blender and purée until smooth. Pour the purée into a cheesecloth-lined fine-mesh sieve and let the juice drain into a bowl until you have the required amount.

PLUM AND LEMONGRASS REFRESHER

— MAKES 1 COCKTAIL —

This cocktail smells almost as good as it tastes. Alongside the light, lemony fragrance of lemongrass and its earthy undertones, the mighty plum brings flavour that's invigorating but doesn't compete with the herb's natural aromatics. Adjust the amount of simple syrup depending on how much sweetness the plum juice lends. The lemongrass tea on its own is a great alcohol-free drink to serve over ice on a hot summer day.

FOR THE LEMONGRASS TEA
(MAKES 3 CUPS, ENOUGH FOR
24 COCKTAILS)

3 cups water
2 stalks lemongrass, cut into 1-inch
    pieces
2 orange pekoe tea bags

FOR THE COCKTAIL

1 ounce gin
1 ounce fresh plum juice
    (about 2 plums; see Bar Tip)
1 ounce lemongrass tea
¾ ounce simple syrup (page 240)
4 dashes lemon bitters
Handful of ice cubes, more for serving
Fresh mint leaf and a lemon wedge,
    for garnish

1. Brew the lemongrass tea. In a small pot, bring the water to a boil. Stir in the lemongrass and tea bags. Remove the pot from the heat and let steep for 10 minutes. Strain the tea through a fine-mesh sieve and let cool before you transfer it to an airtight jar. The tea can be stored in the refrigerator for up to 1 week.

2. Make the cocktail. Add the gin, plum juice, lemongrass tea, syrup, and bitters to a cocktail shaker. Add the ice and shake for 10 to 15 seconds.

3. Strain the cocktail into a highball glass filled with fresh ice cubes, and garnish with mint leaf and a lemon wedge.

Bar Tip: If you don't have a juicer, remove the pits from the plums and cut each plum into quarters. Add them to a blender and purée until smooth. Pour the purée into a cheesecloth-lined fine-mesh sieve and let the juice drain into a bowl until you have the required amount.

PEACHY KEEN

....

We created this cocktail to take advantage of the ripe peaches we pick just down the road from the distillery. The combination of the warm spice notes from the rye, the sweetness from the amaretto and peaches, plus a little kick of heat from the mole bitters makes this a perfectly balanced cocktail. If you prefer a little less sweetness, replace the peach syrup with 1 ounce fresh peach juice.

FOR THE PEACH SYRUP
(MAKES 2 CUPS, ENOUGH
FOR 16 COCKTAILS)

....

½ cup granulated sugar

1 cup water

1 cup fresh peach juice
(3 to 4 peaches; see Bar Tip)

FOR THE COCKTAIL

....

1½ ounces rye whisky

1 ounce peach syrup

1 ounce fresh lemon juice

½ ounce amaretto

2 dashes mole bitters

Handful of ice cubes, more for serving

Peach slice, for garnish

1. Make the peach syrup. Combine the sugar and water in a medium pot and bring to a boil. Reduce the heat to a simmer, stirring until the sugar has dissolved. Remove the pot from the heat and let cool to room temperature.

2. Stir in the peach juice. Transfer the syrup to an airtight container. The syrup will keep in the refrigerator for up to 2 weeks.

3. Make the cocktail. Add the rye whisky, syrup, lemon juice, amaretto, and bitters to a cocktail shaker. Add the ice and shake for 10 to 15 seconds.

4. Strain the cocktail into a highball glass filled with fresh ice. Garnish with a slice of peach.

Bar Tip: If you don't have a juicer, remove the pits from the peaches and cut each peach into quarters. Add them to a blender and purée until smooth. Pour the purée into a cheesecloth-lined fine-mesh sieve and let the juice drain into a bowl until you have the required amount.

WATERMELON COLLINS

— MAKES 1 COCKTAIL —

Watermelon and mint is one of the most refreshing combinations in the summer months. The shrub in this cocktail brings the crisp acidity the drink needs to balance the sweetness from the fresh watermelon. We've included some tips for making shrubs in the Handcrafted Cocktail Staples section (page 244). There are a number of new small producers of shrubs whose goods can almost certainly be found in a specialty food store near you. Give one a try when you're tight on time.

FOR THE WATERMELON SHRUB (MAKES ABOUT 2½ CUPS, ENOUGH FOR 16 COCKTAILS)

2 cups fresh watermelon juice (about ½ small to medium size watermelon; see Bar Tip)

¾ cup white wine vinegar

½ cup granulated sugar

FOR THE COCKTAIL

8 mint leaves, more for garnish

1½ ounces gin

1¼ ounces watermelon shrub

3 dashes hot pepper bitters or other spicy bitters

Handful of ice cubes, more for serving

1 ounce soda water

1. Make the watermelon shrub. Combine the watermelon juice, white wine vinegar, and sugar in a large mason jar. Screw the lid on and shake vigorously for about 30 seconds, or until the sugar has dissolved. Leave the shrub at room temperature overnight, with the lid on.

2. Make the cocktail. Add the mint leaves to a cocktail shaker and muddle lightly. Add the gin, shrub, and bitters. Add the ice and shake for 10 to 15 seconds.

3. Strain the cocktail into a highball glass filled with fresh ice. Top with the soda water and garnish with mint.

Bar Tip: If you don't have a juicer, cut away and discard the rind from the watermelon, then cut the flesh into 2-inch pieces. Add them to a blender and purée until smooth. Pour the purée into a cheesecloth-lined fine-mesh sieve and let the juice drain into a bowl until you have the required amount.

THE GOLDEN HORSESHOE

— MAKES 1 COCKTAIL —

Kevin Delaney competed in the Dillon's Cocktail Cup and won his round with this riff on a Ramos Gin Fizz. When he isn't competing in cocktail competitions or working on his novel, Kevin can be found behind the bar at one of Hamilton, Ontario's coolest spots, Brux House, mixing drinks and making friends. We love cocktails that incorporate beer because it adds layers of flavour and a bit more character.

4 or 5 peach slices, more for garnish

2 ounces Dillon's Black Walnut Amaro
    or amaro of choice

1 bottle IPA beer, divided

1 ounce fresh lemon juice

1 ounce simple syrup (page 240)

1 ounce half-and-half (10%) cream

½ ounce egg white

3 dashes wormwood bitters

Handful of ice cubes

1. Add the peaches and amaro to a Boston shaker and muddle. Add 1 ounce of the beer, the lemon juice, syrup, cream, egg white, and bitters. Add the ice and shake well for 10 to 15 seconds.

2. Strain the cocktail through a fine-mesh sieve into the larger half of the Boston shaker and then back into the smaller half. Discard the ice. Shake the cocktail a second time without ice for 15 to 20 seconds (this is called a dry shake).

3. Pour the cocktail into a highball glass. Let the cocktail sit for 20 to 30 seconds, until the egg white and cream solidify into a rich meringue.

4. Top up the cocktail with IPA. If you've given the cocktail enough time to rest, the rich head will rise up above the rim of the glass. Garnish with peach slices.

Bar Tip: One large egg yields approximately 1 ounce egg white.

MOSCOW MULE

— MAKES 1 COCKTAIL —

A Moscow Mule will quench your thirst on the hottest of summer days. The spicy taste of ginger mixed with the lime's tartness, along with loads of ice, goes down easy and has us longing for a patio. Craving a twist on the old favourite? Impress your friends by using whatever fresh fruit or herbs you have on hand. You might try muddling a few fresh cherries in the shaker with the vodka and lime juice. Strawberries and a small handful of mint work well too—or maybe you prefer the combination of raspberries and basil, or the Mexican flavours of hot pepper and cilantro. Take your pick!

2 ounces vodka

½ ounce fresh lime juice

2 dashes lime bitters

Ice cubes, for serving

4 ounces Ginger Beer
(page 246; see Bar Tip)

Lime wheel, for garnish

1. Place a copper mug in the freezer to chill at least 1 hour before you plan to serve the cocktail.

2. Once the mug is nice and cold, add the vodka, lime juice, and bitters. Fill the mug with ice and top with Ginger Beer.

3. Give the cocktail a quick stir to combine all the ingredients, and garnish with a lime wheel.

Bar Tip: If you don't have a batch of your own homemade Ginger Beer on hand, and don't have time to make some, any non-alcoholic ginger beer from the market will do the trick here—so no pressure.

WILD BLUEBERRY GIN PUNCH

······················

Did you ever sneak a spoonful or two of pie filling when baking with your parents or grandparents when you were young? With its combination of fresh blueberries and lemon juice, drinking this cocktail is just as delicious and just as satisfying as diving into the blueberry filling moments before the pie goes into the oven. While they're not always as easy to find as regular blueberries, wild blueberries explode with flavour, so they're worth hunting down. If you can't find wild blueberries, cultivated blueberries bring their own robust flavour. This would be a great cocktail to kick off your next garden party. Serve it in a beautiful glass drink dispenser to make being a host a little bit less stressful.

1 cup fresh wild blueberries,
    more for garnish

⅓ cup fresh lemon juice

½ cup granulated sugar

¼ cup water

25 to 30 fresh pineapple mint leaves
    (about ½ cup firmly packed),
    more for garnish

1¼ cups dry gin

½ (25-ounce/750 mL) bottle dry
    sparkling wine

1. In a medium pot, combine the blueberries, lemon juice, sugar, and water. Bring the mixture to a boil. Reduce the heat to a simmer, stirring until the sugar has dissolved. Muddle the berries, add the pineapple mint, and continue to simmer for 2 minutes.

2. Remove the pot from the heat and let steep for several hours. The longer it sits, the more mint flavour will come through.

3. Strain the blueberry mixture through a fine-mesh sieve into a large punch bowl or glass drink dispenser with a spigot, pressing down hard on the berries with the back of a spoon to release as much of their colourful juice as possible.

4. Add the gin and sparkling wine and stir to combine. Garnish with a few extra mint leaves and blueberries. Serve in stemmed wine glasses.

Bar Tip: 1. Make a giant ice cube (using a metal or silicone loaf pan and freezing overnight) to place in the punch bowl or dispenser. A large ice cube will keep the punch cold without watering it down too quickly. 2. If you can't find pineapple mint, use classic mint, or substitute basil.

NIAGARA PALOMA

— MAKES 1 COCKTAIL —

A Paloma is a traditional Mexican cocktail prepared with tequila. But here we give it local flair with our unaged grain spirit, The White Rye. Some recipes call for sparkling grapefruit soda, but we use fresh grapefruit juice and soda water. To give the cocktail a more complex, spicy taste, use ginger beer in place of the soda water. Ginger and grapefruit work extremely well together, and the saltiness from the rim balances the two bold flavours well.

2 tablespoons kosher salt

Grapefruit wedge, for rimming
and garnish

2 ounces Dillon's The White Rye
or tequila

2 ounces fresh grapefruit juice

½ ounce fresh lime juice

1 teaspoon granulated sugar

3 dashes ginger bitters

Handful of ice cubes, more for serving

2 ounces soda water or Ginger Beer
(page 246; see Bar Tip)

1. Rim the glass. Pour the salt onto a small plate. Wet the rim of a highball glass using the grapefruit wedge, then turn the outside rim of the glass in the salt.

2. Make the cocktail. Add The White Rye or tequila, grapefruit juice, lime juice, sugar, and bitters to a cocktail shaker. Add the ice and shake for 10 to 15 seconds.

3. Fill the rimmed highball glass with fresh ice, then strain the cocktail into it. Top with either soda water or Ginger Beer and garnish with the grapefruit wedge.

Bar Tip: If you don't have a batch of your own homemade Ginger Beer on hand, and don't have time to make some, but prefer that spicy, gingery flavour, any non-alcoholic ginger beer from the market will do the trick here.

PLUM SPARKLER

......

— MAKES 1 COCKTAIL —

The key to this cocktail is making sure that you use ripe, juicy plums. You can use any type of plum you wish, from those that have light golden skin to dark, deep red plums. The cocktail will take on a very different colour depending on the variety of plum you use, but that's part of the fun. Plums and honey along with a bit of tart acidity from citrus juice make for a great combination that everyone will enjoy!

FOR THE RICH HONEY SYRUP
(MAKES 1⅓ CUPS, ENOUGH
FOR 15 COCKTAILS)
......

1 cup pure honey
½ cup water

FOR THE COCKTAIL
......

1 plum, pitted
Pinch of coarse sea salt
1 ounce vodka
¾ ounce rich honey syrup
½ ounce fresh lemon juice
3 dashes pear bitters
Handful of ice cubes
1 ounce soda water

1. Make the rich honey syrup. Combine the honey and water in a small pot and bring to a boil over medium heat, stirring occasionally. Once the honey is incorporated, remove the pot from the heat and let cool for 30 minutes. Transfer the syrup to an airtight container. It will keep in the refrigerator for up to 2 weeks.

2. Make the cocktail. Add the plum and salt to a cocktail shaker and muddle. Add the vodka, syrup, lemon juice, and bitters. Add the ice and shake for 10 to 15 seconds.

3. Strain the cocktail into a coupe glass and top with the soda water.

DILLON'S CAESAR

— MAKES 1 COCKTAIL —

What could be more Canadian than a Caesar? Walter Chell made the first Caesar in Calgary, Alberta, in 1969, and it has since become Canada's national drink. A Caesar has also become the cocktail of choice for Sunday brunch, and in many cases is thought of as "hair of the dog"—an alcoholic hangover cure to imbibe after a few too many drinks the night before. We have trouble choosing a garnish for a Caesar, so we encourage you to think outside the box. Anything from a classic celery stalk to a full lobster tail seems to fit.

FOR THE RIMMER

¼ cup coarse salt

2 tablespoons black pepper

1 tablespoon garlic powder

2 teaspoons chili powder

1 teaspoon dried lemon zest (optional)

½ teaspoon cayenne pepper

FOR THE COCKTAIL

Lime wedge

Ice cubes, for serving

1½ ounces vodka or gin

2 dashes celery bitters

2 dashes hot pepper bitters

2 dashes Worcestershire sauce

1 teaspoon grated fresh horseradish, or to taste

4 ounces tomato-clam juice

GARNISHES (OPTIONAL)

Celery stalk

Citrus wheel

Pickles or Quick Pickled Onion (page 248)

Skewered shrimp

Bacon

Oysters

1. Make the rimmer. To an airtight jar, add the salt, black pepper, garlic powder, chili powder, dried lemon zest (if using), and cayenne pepper. Stir well. The rimmer can be stored for up to 6 months.

2. Rim the glass. Pour the rimmer onto a small plate. Wet the rim of a highball glass using the lime wedge, then turn the outside rim of the glass in the rimmer.

3. Make the cocktail. Add the ice to the rimmed glass. Pour in the vodka or gin, celery bitters, hot pepper bitters, Worcestershire sauce, and fresh horseradish.

4. Top with the tomato-clam juice, and stir to combine. Garnish with your choice of accoutrement.

Bar Tip: 1. If you have a Caesar lover in your life, make a large batch of rimmer and package it in a mason jar with a handmade label as a gift. 2. If you are serving a vegan or someone who's not a fan of the clam flavour in tomato-clam juice, substitute Clarified Tomato Water (page 247). It gives the finished cocktail a different, clear appearance.

THE MARIPOSA FLOAT

Mariposa isn't so much a place as a lifestyle. Our photographer, Nataschia, lives on one of the prettiest streets you will ever see, where the neighbours enjoy porch drinks and kids play outside until after the street lights come on. This cocktail was inspired by the so-called Mariposa life, and it is perfect for a hot summer day. The combination of fresh peach flavours and vanilla ice cream makes this the ultimate cool-down cocktail.

16 peach slices

12 ounces peach schnapps

8 scoops vanilla bean ice cream

24 ounces dry sparkling wine

1. Place 2 peach slices in each of 8 wine glasses. Add 1½ ounces peach schnapps to each glass, followed by 1 scoop of vanilla ice cream.

2. Top each cocktail with 3 ounces sparkling wine.

APERITIVO SPRITZ

— MAKES 1 COCKTAIL —

A classic spritz calls for just an orange slice as a garnish, but we have taken some summer-inspired liberties, adding some fresh blackberries and basil from the garden. The basil helps to elevate the character and aroma of the spritz, giving it an herbal note that is new.

Handful of ice cubes

3 ounces dry sparkling wine

2 ounces Aperol or bitter aperitivo
    of choice

½ ounce soda water

3 dashes orange bitters

Garnishes: orange slice, blackberries,
    and fresh basil sprig

1. Fill a wine glass with ice cubes. Add the sparkling wine, Aperol or aperitivo, soda water, and bitters. Stir to combine.

2. Garnish with an orange slice, blackberries, and basil.

Bar Tip: To add a fresh dark-berry flavour to the cocktail, muddle 2 blackberries in your wine glass before adding the ice and other ingredients.

STRAWBERRY GIN SHAVED ICE

— SERVES 8 —

Spirits aren't just for cocktails. They make a pretty wonderful ingredient in the kitchen too, thanks to their abundance of flavour. We have used a traditional dry gin for this recipe, but if you happen to have a bottle of Dillon's Strawberry Gin, use it in place of the dry gin for even more intense strawberry flavour. This shaved ice is easy to make—just make sure you leave enough time for the prep work. As a warning: you might also have some trouble sharing it with your guests when it's ready. It's really that good!

3 cups strawberries, hulled and halved

1 cup water

½ cup granulated sugar

2 teaspoons lime zest (about 1 lime)

2 tablespoons lime juice (about 1 lime)

1 cup tonic water

¼ cup dry gin

8 fresh mint leaves, for garnish (optional)

1. Combine the strawberries, water, sugar, lime zest, and lime juice in a medium pot and bring to a boil over medium heat. Reduce the heat and simmer until the strawberries are completely soft, 5 to 8 minutes. Remove the pot from the heat and let cool to room temperature.

2. In a blender, purée the mixture until smooth. Add the tonic water and gin, and stir to combine.

3. Pour the liquid into a 9-inch square metal baking pan and place it in the freezer for 2 to 3 hours.

4. Once frozen, scrape the strawberry mixture with a fork until the texture resembles coarse crystals. Return the pan to the freezer for an hour, then scrape again. Cover with plastic wrap and keep frozen for up to 3 days.

5. Scrape the shaved ice into small bowls and garnish with mint, if desired.

Roasted Beet and Lemon Hummus

— Serves 4 to 6 —

Who doesn't love anything that comes in dip form? And the colour, oh, the colour! This dip is sure to brighten up any table. We are big fans of the lemon juice in this recipe. The fresh acidity it brings helps to liven up the hummus and give it a clean, light finish. Entertaining should be easy for every host, and this hummus can be made ahead of time (even the day before) and kept in the refrigerator until it is time to serve. Perfect paired with Summer Sangria (page 103), or keep the beet theme rolling with a Beet Ya To It (page 95).

2 medium beets, unpeeled

1 baguette

¼ cup + 2 tablespoons extra-virgin olive oil

1 (15-ounce/425 g) can chickpeas, rinsed and drained

2 tablespoons fresh lemon juice

2 tablespoons tahini

2 garlic cloves, pressed or minced

1 teaspoon sea salt

½ teaspoon smoked paprika

¼ teaspoon chili flakes

3 or 4 dashes lemon bitters (optional)

1 to 2 tablespoons olive oil (optional)

Crackers, for serving (optional)

GARNISHES (OPTIONAL)

Drizzle of olive oil

2 tablespoons chopped fresh dill

¼ cup crumbled feta cheese

Lemon slices (about ½ lemon)

¼ cup crushed pistachios

1. Preheat the oven to 400°F. Grease a small baking dish or pot.

2. Rinse the beets. Pierce them a few times with a fork and place them in the baking dish. Cover with foil and roast until tender, 45 to 60 minutes. Set aside to cool.

3. Slice the baguette, arrange the slices on a baking sheet, and drizzle them with the olive oil. Bake for 10 minutes, or until golden brown and crisp. Let cool.

4. When the beets are cool enough to handle, peel them using your hands or a vegetable peeler. Dice the beets.

5. To a food processor, add the beets, chickpeas, lemon juice, tahini, garlic, sea salt, paprika, chili flakes, and bitters, if desired. Purée until smooth. If needed, pulse in 1 to 2 tablespoons olive oil, a little at a time, until you reach the desired consistency.

6. Serve in a wide, shallow bowl, with the garnishes of your choice alongside the toasted baguette slices and crackers, if desired.

Cheese and Charcuterie Board

— Serves 6 to 8 —

A fancy cheese and charcuterie board is welcome at any party, especially one where cocktails are involved. This board would be a great accompaniment to any of the light spritz-like cocktails in the book, such as the Aperitivo Spritz (page 124), Moscow Mule (page 112), or even a glass of whisky neat. Find your own match made in heaven for a chill summer gathering.

¾ pound blue cheese

¾ pound triple-crème Brie

½ pound Oka-style cheese

1 pound three-year-old cheddar

1 pound prosciutto, thinly sliced

1 pound salami, thinly sliced

1 pound soppressata, thinly sliced

Quick Pickled Onions (page 248)

½ cup dried apricots

¼ cup pitted Medjool dates

¼ cup Kalamata olives

¼ cup Manzanilla olives

½ cup Rosemary Maple Pecans
    (page 179) or raw walnuts

Crackers or crisps

½ baguette, sliced

1. Select a large platter or wine barrel stave serving board to present the ingredients.

2. Arrange the blue cheese, brie, Oka-style cheese, and aged cheddar around the board.

3. Place the prosciutto, salami, and soppressata in small piles on the board as well.

4. Fill in the gaps with the Quick Pickled Onions, apricots, dates, olives, and nuts.

5. Finally, arrange the crackers and baguette slices around the board, and serve the mouth-watering board to your guests.

GOURMET GROWN-UP POPCORN, TWO WAYS

— EACH BOWL OF POPCORN SERVES 2 TO 4 —

Popcorn brings back so many memories of being young and watching movies or sitting around the campfire. Now that we've all grown up a little, we thought it only appropriate to serve some "classed-up" popcorn with toppings that would go great alongside your favourite cocktail. To complement the salty nature of the suggested toppings below, we suggest serving the popcorn alongside a slightly sweeter cocktail, like the Peachy Keen (page 107) or Berry Bramble (page 87).

CILANTRO LIME POPCORN

1 tablespoon canola oil

¼ cup popcorn kernels

2 tablespoons butter

1 tablespoon lime juice (about ½ lime)

¼ cup fresh cilantro, chopped

1 teaspoon fine sea salt

LEMON, PARMESAN, AND BLACK PEPPERCORN POPCORN

1 tablespoon canola oil

¼ cup popcorn kernels

Finely grated zest of 1 small lemon

¼ cup finely grated Parmesan cheese

Fine sea salt

Freshly cracked black pepper

1. Heat the canola oil in a medium heavy-bottomed pot over medium heat. Add a few popcorn kernels and cover the pot while it heats up. When you hear one kernel pop, add the rest of the kernels and cover the pot. Shake the pot from side to side a few times to spread the kernels in an even layer.

2. Let the kernels pop for several minutes until the popping slows down, shaking the pot often to ensure the kernels don't burn. When there are about 4 or 5 seconds between each pop, remove the pot from the heat and transfer the popcorn to a large bowl.

3. For the cilantro lime popcorn, melt the butter in a small pot over medium heat. Once the butter has melted, remove the pot from the heat and stir in the lime juice and cilantro. Drizzle the mixture over the popcorn and toss to coat evenly. Sprinkle with the salt.

4. For the lemon, Parmesan, and black peppercorn popcorn, sprinkle the lemon zest and Parmesan over the popcorn and gently toss to combine. Add salt and pepper to taste.

FALL

The start of the cooler months means fall flavours start to emerge and we start crafting deeper, richer-tasting cocktails. But even with a shift in temperatures this time of year, we still find plums available at some farm stands, plus all the quintessential fall fruits like apples, pears, and even black walnuts, which we pick just down the road from the distillery. Fall is also the time of year to harvest botanicals from the garden to make absinthe. At the distillery we grow our own wormwood, lemon balm, and hyssop that go into crafting Dillon's Absinthe (page 16), and these make a world of difference in the finished spirit. With the cool breezes of fall come cocktails that warm you from the inside, like the BFF: Best Fronds Forever (page 156), the Beam Bulldog (page 160), and especially Mulled Rye Cider (page 147).

COCKTAILS

SNACKS

No Fixed Address

Fall gives us rich and hearty cocktails, and this one by Ian Storcer of Proof Cocktail Bar, in Calgary, Alberta, is no exception. With the warm spice of cinnamon and a barrel-aged fruit spirit, this drink serves the full essence of fall in a single glass. Enjoy this cocktail while watching the leaves change colour on your porch on Thanksgiving weekend, or up at the cottage as the cooler weather starts to set in.

FOR THE CINNAMON SYRUP
(MAKES ABOUT 1 CUP,
ENOUGH FOR 10 COCKTAILS)

¾ cup water
1 (3-inch) cinnamon stick
½ cup granulated sugar

FOR THE COCKTAIL

1 ounce dry gin
1 ounce pear brandy
¾ ounce fresh lemon juice
¾ ounce cinnamon syrup
2 dashes orange bitters
Handful of ice cubes
Fresh rosemary sprig, for garnish

1. Make the cinnamon syrup. Combine the water and cinnamon sticks in a medium pot and bring to a boil over medium-high heat. Boil for 10 to 15 minutes, until the liquid is reduced by about one-third. Stir in the sugar, and continue to stir until it has dissolved, another 2 to 3 minutes. Remove the pot from the heat and let cool for at least 30 minutes.

2. Strain the syrup into an airtight container. The syrup will keep in the refrigerator for up to 2 weeks.

3. Make the cocktail. Add the gin, brandy, lemon juice, syrup, and bitters to a cocktail shaker. Add the ice and shake for 10 to 15 seconds.

4. Strain the cocktail into a coupe glass and garnish with a rosemary sprig.

THE HARVEST GOLD

— MAKES 1 COCKTAIL —

When you feel that first chill in the air and summer turns to fall, this drink will help to ease the transition. With its fresh plums and pear bitters, some might classify this as a summer cocktail, but the sage-infused syrup conjures fall with its earthy flavour. If you can't get your hands on ripe plums, use some farm-crafted plum jam instead—just remember to use half the amount of sage syrup to ensure the drink isn't too sweet.

FOR THE SAGE SYRUP
(MAKES ¾ CUP, ENOUGH
FOR 12 COCKTAILS)

½ cup granulated sugar
½ cup water
4 or 5 fresh sage leaves

FOR THE COCKTAIL

1½ ounces fresh golden plum purée
      (2 to 3 plums; see Bar Tip)
1 ounce vodka
½ ounce sage syrup
½ ounce fresh lemon juice
4 dashes pear bitters
Handful of ice cubes
1 ounce soda water
Fresh sage leaf, for garnish

1. Make the sage syrup. Combine the sugar, water, and sage leaves in a small pot and bring to a boil. Reduce the heat to a simmer, stirring until the sugar has dissolved. Remove the pot from the heat and let cool to room temperature.

2. Strain the syrup into an airtight container. The syrup will keep in the refrigerator for up to 2 weeks.

3. Make the cocktail. Add the plum purée, vodka, syrup, lemon juice, and bitters to a cocktail shaker. Add the ice and shake for 10 to 15 seconds.

4. Strain the cocktail into a coupe glass and top with soda water. Garnish with a sage leaf.

Bar Tip: To make the plum purée, peel and pit the plums and cut into quarters. Add the plums to a blender and purée until smooth, adding 1 to 2 teaspoons of water if needed. Transfer to a jar, cover, and refrigerate for up to 3 days.

WEEKEND IN NIAGARA

— MAKES 1 COCKTAIL —

A twist on the Roman Holiday, this cocktail came out of our desire for a cocktail that was light and refreshing but still featured amaro front and centre. Here, bitter and sweet flavours combine in perfect harmony thanks to the addition of the vermouth. We use peach bitters in this recipe, but you could easily substitute ginger bitters or aromatic bitters. This may be one of the last times to use fresh mint from the garden before the first frost sets in.

1½ ounces amaro

¾ ounce fresh lemon juice

½ ounce sweet vermouth

¼ ounce simple syrup (page 240)

2 dashes peach bitters

Handful of ice cubes, more for serving

1 ounce soda water (optional)

Fresh mint sprig, for garnish

1. Add the amaro, lemon juice, vermouth, syrup, and bitters to a cocktail shaker. Add the ice and shake for 10 to 15 seconds.

2. Strain the cocktail into a rocks glass filled with fresh ice cubes. Top with soda water and garnish with mint.

FIGGIN' LOVE YOU

— Makes 1 cocktail —

Figs are one of those ingredients that we don't use often, but when we have a chance to include them in a cocktail, they never disappoint. Even though it's fall, we still love a clean and refreshing cocktail, and the mix of fig, vodka, and fresh lemon juice gives us just that. We use dehydrated fig slices to garnish this drink, but a slice of fresh fig would look just as stunning in your finished cocktail.

FOR THE FIG SYRUP
(MAKES ¾ CUP, ENOUGH
FOR 8 COCKTAILS)
....···........

½ cup granulated sugar
½ cup water
5 fresh figs, quartered

FOR THE COCKTAIL
....···........

1 ounce vodka
¾ ounce fig syrup
½ ounce fresh lemon juice
3 dashes aromatic bitters
Handful of ice cubes
1 (2-inch-square) ice cube, for serving
½ to 1 ounce soda water (optional)
Dehydrated fig slice (page 250),
    for garnish

1. Make the fig syrup. Combine the sugar, water, and figs in a small pot and bring to a boil. Reduce the heat to a simmer, stirring until the sugar has dissolved and the figs begin to break down, about 5 minutes. Remove the pot from the heat and let cool for at least 30 minutes, pressing on the figs as they cool to extract all the flavour.

2. Strain the syrup through a fine-mesh sieve into an airtight container. The syrup will keep in the refrigerator for up to 2 weeks.

3. Make the cocktail. Add the vodka, syrup, lemon juice, and bitters to a cocktail shaker. Add the ice and shake for 10 to 15 seconds.

4. Strain the cocktail into a rocks glass over a large ice cube. Top with soda water (if using) and garnish with a dehydrated fig slice.

CHANNEL ORANGE

— MAKES 1 COCKTAIL —

As the weather starts to cool off we cling to as many clean, fresh, and almost summer-like cocktails as we can. This one, created by Joanna Matysiak of the restaurant La Carnita, in Toronto, is no exception. By using a more aromatic and floral-forward gin, Joanna has found a way to offer a vibrant yet restrained amount of orange and floral notes, and balanced it expertly with the sweetness of the Lillet Blanc. Her recipe calls for a Nick and Nora glass, a variation on the classic coupe glass, but if you don't have one, feel free to bust out your favourite vintage coupe glass for this one.

FOR THE ORANGE BLOSSOM
HONEY SYRUP (MAKES 1¾ CUPS,
ENOUGH FOR 14 COCKTAILS)

1 cup pure honey

1 cup water

1 ounce orange blossom water

FOR THE COCKTAIL

1½ ounces gin

1 ounce orange blossom honey syrup

1 ounce fresh lime juice

½ ounce Lillet Blanc

2 dashes orange bitters

Handful of ice cubes

Orange zest, for garnish

1. Make the orange blossom honey syrup. Combine the honey and water in a small pot and bring to a boil over medium heat, stirring until the honey has fully incorporated. Remove the pot from the heat and stir in the orange blossom water. Let the mixture cool to room temperature. The syrup can be stored in a sealed mason jar in the refrigerator for up to 2 weeks.

2. Make the cocktail. Add the gin, syrup, lime juice, Lillet Blanc, and bitters to a cocktail shaker. Add the ice and shake well for 10 to 15 seconds.

3. Strain the cocktail into a Nick and Nora glass. Garnish with the orange zest.

Bar Tip: Orange blossom water is distilled from bitter-orange blossoms. It is clear in colour and offers a delicate orange scent to cocktails. It can be found at most specialty food stores and many large supermarkets as well.

MULLED RYE CIDER

....

We first served this cocktail at an outdoor event that takes place each year at the distillery when the weather starts to chill. Since we knew we would be serving cocktails outdoors, we imagined everyone would be grateful for something warm. They were, and we continue to make and enjoy this cocktail every fall—and even through the winter months too. It's that good. It's also a cocktail that travels well, so it would make a great addition to a picnic at the end of a brisk fall hike.

FOR THE MULLING SPICE
....

1 tablespoon whole allspice

1 tablespoon whole cloves

4 whole star anise

3 (3-inch) cinnamon sticks

2 tablespoons orange zest
(about 1 medium orange)

2 (½-inch) slices peeled fresh ginger

FOR THE COCKTAILS
....

4 cups fresh-pressed apple cider

Mulling spice

1½ cups rye whisky

30 dashes aromatic bitters

Garnishes: 8 apple slices and
8 (2-inch) cinnamon sticks

1. Make the mulling spice. In a jar, combine the allspice, cloves, star anise, cinnamon sticks, orange zest, and ginger. Store at room temperature until ready to use.

2. Make the cocktails. Combine the cider and all the mulling spice in a large pot. Bring to a boil over medium heat. Reduce the heat to a bare simmer, keeping the cider warm until you serve the cocktails.

3. To each of 8 mugs or heatproof glasses, add 1½ ounces rye and then the warm cider mixture. Garnish each drink with an apple slice and cinnamon stick.

THE SPOILT ONE

— MAKES 1 COCKTAIL —

This recipe was contributed by Adam Hynam-Smith, co-owner and executive chef at Dispatch restaurant, in St. Catharines, Ontario. Tepache, a fermented beverage originally from Mexico, should be started at least a week in advance, as it requires time to ferment. If making the tepache from scratch seems like a lot of work, replace it with 2 ounces pineapple juice and 1 ounce Ginger Beer (page 246 or store-bought) and start the recipe at step 8.

FOR THE PINEAPPLE TEPACHE (MAKES ABOUT 4½ CUPS, ENOUGH FOR 12 COCKTAILS)

1 pineapple

1¼ cups loosely packed dark brown sugar or piloncillo

½ cup (¼-inch) slices unpeeled fresh ginger

1 habanero pepper, seeded

3⅓ cups distilled water

3 ounces ginger kombucha

FOR THE RICH HONEY SYRUP (MAKES ABOUT 1⅓ CUPS, ENOUGH FOR 20 COCKTAILS)

1 cup pure honey

½ cup water

FOR THE COCKTAIL

1½ ounces rye whisky

½ ounce rich honey syrup

2 dashes aromatic bitters

Ice cubes

1 (2-inch-square) ice cube, for serving

3 ounces pineapple tepache

Pineapple leaf, for garnish

1. Make the pineapple tepache. Slice off the top and bottom of the pineapple, but leave the skin on. Reserve the pineapple leaves for garnishing your cocktail. Quarter the pineapple lengthwise and cut out the core. Cut the pineapple quarters into 1-inch cubes.

2. Working in batches, purée the pineapple, brown sugar, ginger, and habanero in a food processor. The purée does not need to be smooth, but can remain chunky.

3. In a large bowl, stir together the pineapple purée, distilled water, and kombucha. Pour the mixture into a sterilized large fermenting jar (or divide it among clean mason jars). Cover the top of the fermenting jar with folded cheesecloth and secure it with an elastic band. Leave the mixture to ferment for at least 4 days in a warm, dry area of the kitchen that has a little airflow.

4. Each day, uncover the jar to admire the fermenting action, and to "punch down" the mixture: using a sterilized stainless steel spoon or ladle, press the pulp that is sitting on top down to the bottom of the jar. You will see an explosion of bubbles rise to the surface. These bubbles will subside as fermentation proceeds. On the fourth day, taste the juice. It will taste drier as the fermentation goes on, so you may decide to finish it whenever the desired flavour profile is reached. Feel free to add more sugar if you desire a sweeter finish.

5.   Strain the tepache through a fine-mesh sieve into a pot without pressing on the tepache. You want a pulp-free liquid. Strain it again, this time through a fine-mesh sieve lined with cheesecloth and allowing the liquid to gently flow through at its own pace.

6.   Using a funnel, transfer the tepache to clean plastic soda bottles with screw tops. Cap the bottles tightly and refrigerate for 2 days to allow for a second fermentation.

7.   When opening a bottle, be very careful, as a lot of pressure may have built up and it may foam out for a little bit. If this occurs, let the bottle rest in the sink until the fizzing subsides.

8.   Make the rich honey syrup. Combine the honey and water in a small pot. Bring to a boil over medium-high heat, stirring until honey is fully incorporated. Remove the pot from the heat and allow to cool for at least 30 minutes. Transfer it to an airtight container. The syrup will keep in the refrigerator for up to 2 weeks.

9.   Make the cocktail. Add the rye whisky, syrup, and bitters to a cocktail shaker. Add the ice and shake for 10 to 15 seconds.

10.   Strain the cocktail into a rocks glass over a large ice cube. Top with the tepache and garnish with a pineapple leaf.

MANHATTAN

— MAKES 1 COCKTAIL —

There isn't a cocktail more classic than a Manhattan. With its simple ingredients, it's also one that any home cocktail enthusiast can master easily. Since we love Manhattans so much, and since the cherry garnish is such a big part of the cocktail, we have included a recipe to make your own Whisky-Soaked Cherries at home.

2 ounces rye whisky

1 ounce sweet vermouth

2 dashes aromatic bitters

Handful of ice cubes

1 (2-inch-square) ice cube, for serving
    (optional)

Whisky-Soaked Cherries (page 249),
    for garnish

1. Add the whisky, vermouth, and bitters to a mixing glass. Add the ice cubes and stir for 20 to 30 seconds.

2. Strain the cocktail into a rocks glass over a large ice cube (if using), or serve neat in a short-stemmed martini glass. Garnish with a couple of Whisky-Soaked Cherries.

PUMPKIN SPICE OLD-FASHIONED

— MAKES 1 COCKTAIL —

If you're a purist when it comes to old-fashioneds, this recipe might seem a bit of a stretch to you, but nothing says fall quite like pumpkins and warm spices. In this take on the classic old-fashioned, the pumpkin spice syrup brings sweetness to the drink in place of the usual sugar cube; the cocktail remains perfectly balanced, but with a different and satisfying depth of flavour.

FOR THE PUMPKIN SPICE SYRUP (MAKES ABOUT 1½ CUPS, ENOUGH FOR 24 COCKTAILS)

....

1½ cups water

1 cup granulated sugar

½ cup loosely packed dark brown sugar

½ teaspoon ground ginger

½ teaspoon nutmeg

½ teaspoon ground cloves

¼ cup canned pumpkin purée

4 cinnamon sticks

FOR THE COCKTAIL

....

2 ounces rye whisky

½ ounce Grand Marnier

½ ounce pumpkin spice syrup

2 dashes aromatic bitters

Handful of ice cubes

1 (2-inch-square) ice cube, for serving

Orange zest and freshly grated nutmeg, for garnish

1. Make the pumpkin spice syrup. Combine the water, granulated sugar, and brown sugar in a small pot and bring to a boil, stirring until the sugar dissolves. Reduce the heat to a simmer, add the ginger, nutmeg, cloves, and pumpkin purée, and whisk vigorously until well combined. Add the cinnamon sticks and simmer for 7 minutes, stirring every few minutes. Remove the pot from the heat and let cool for at least 30 minutes.

2. Strain the mixture through a fine-mesh sieve into an airtight container. The syrup will keep in the refrigerator for up to 2 weeks.

3. Make the cocktail. Add the whisky, Grand Marnier, syrup, and bitters to a mixing glass. Add the ice cubes and stir for 20 to 30 seconds.

4. Strain the cocktail into a rocks glass over a large ice cube. Garnish with the orange zest and freshly grated nutmeg.

BOWES PEARS 1929

....

The pear trees on our friend Torrie Warner's farm were planted all the way back in 1929 by a Mr. Bowes, making them some of the oldest pear trees in the town of Lincoln, Ontario. This cocktail is an ode to Mr. Bowes and his mouth-watering pears. Most of the time we use Bartlett pears in cocktails, as they are a bit juicier than other varieties when ripe. Bosc pears have a slight spicy flavour that complements their sweet taste and would work well in this cocktail too. Pear and vanilla seem like such a natural fit and the combination brings warmth to the drink, while the subtle hint of citrus from the lemon juice and orange bitters balances the sweetness of the vanilla bean.

¼ cup granulated sugar

Seeds of 1 vanilla bean, divided

3 ounces fresh pear juice
    (about 1½ ripe pears; see Bar Tip)

1½ ounces vodka

¼ ounce fresh lemon juice

3 dashes orange bitters

Handful of ice cubes, more for serving

1 ounce soda water (optional)

Pear slice, for garnish

1. Rim the glass. Pour the sugar onto a small plate. Add half of the vanilla seeds and mix together until the vanilla is evenly distributed throughout the sugar. Dip the rim of a rocks glass into a shallow bowl of water. Roll the outside rim of the glass in the sugar mixture.

2. Make the cocktail. Add the pear juice, vodka, lemon juice, bitters, and remaining vanilla seeds to a cocktail shaker. Add the ice and shake for 10 to 15 seconds, until well chilled.

3. Fill the rimmed glass with fresh ice cubes. Strain the cocktail into the glass and top with soda water, if desired. Garnish with a pear slice.

Bar Tip: If you don't have a juicer, core the pears and cut into large chunks. Add the pears to a blender and purée until smooth. Pour the purée into a cheesecloth-lined fine-mesh sieve and let the juice drain into a bowl until you have the required amount.

BFF: Best Fronds Forever

— Makes 1 cocktail —

There is something both odd and special about this cocktail's combination of floral notes from the gin and savoury flavours of the anise and salt. If you don't have green Chartreuse at home, you can use ¼ ounce of absinthe in its place. Absinthe will give the cocktail a more pronounced anise flavour, but since anise is the dominant flavour here, why not go all in?

FOR THE LEMON THYME SYRUP (MAKES ABOUT ¾ CUP, ENOUGH FOR 12 COCKTAILS)

½ cup granulated sugar

½ cup water

½ large lemon, sliced

1 fresh thyme sprig

FOR THE COCKTAIL

1 (2-inch) piece fennel stalk

4 fresh sage leaves, more for garnish

Pinch of sea salt

1½ ounces dry gin

½ ounce green Chartreuse

½ ounce fresh lemon juice

½ ounce lemon thyme syrup

4 dashes wormwood bitters

Handful of ice cubes

Fennel frond, for garnish

1. Make the lemon thyme syrup. Combine the sugar, water, lemon, and thyme in a medium pot and bring to a boil, stirring occasionally until the sugar has dissolved. Reduce the heat and simmer for 5 minutes. Remove the pot from the heat and let cool for at least 20 minutes.

2. Strain the mixture into an airtight container. The syrup can be stored in the refrigerator for up to 2 weeks.

3. Make the cocktail. Add the fennel, sage, and salt to a cocktail shaker and muddle until they are fragrant and pulpy. Add the gin, green Chartreuse, lemon juice, syrup, and bitters. Add the ice and shake vigorously for 10 to 15 seconds.

4. Double-strain the cocktail into a vintage wine glass and garnish with a fennel frond and some sage leaves.

CONCORD GRAPE AND ORANGECELLO FIZZ

Niagara is known as one of the best grape-growing regions in Canada, if not the world, thanks to its cool climate. Today, most of the vineyards plant vinifera grape varieties such as Riesling, Chardonnay, and Cabernet Franc, but there are still a few Concord grapes growing in the area. Concord grapes are used more often now to make jams and pies, but their juice is stellar in cocktails like this one! This cocktail is our way of giving a tip of the hat to the hard-working grape growers and winemakers we call neighbours. With the combination of the grape syrup and orange liqueur, it is like the grown-up version of an orange Creamsicle.

FOR THE CONCORD SYRUP (MAKES ABOUT 2 CUPS, ENOUGH FOR 16 COCKTAILS)

2 cups Concord grapes

1 cup granulated sugar

1 cup water

FOR THE COCKTAIL

1 ounce vodka

1 ounce orangecello or orange liqueur of choice

1 ounce Concord syrup

2 dashes orange bitters

Handful of ice cubes, more for serving

2 ounces soda water

Fresh thyme bundle, for garnish

1. Make the Concord syrup. Combine the grapes, sugar, and water in a small pot and bring to a boil. Reduce the heat and simmer for 10 minutes, using the back of a spoon to help break down the grapes. Remove the pot from the heat and let cool to room temperature.

2. Strain the syrup into an airtight container. The syrup will keep in the refrigerator for up to 2 weeks.

3. Make the cocktail. Add the vodka, orangecello or orange liqueur, syrup, and bitters to a cocktail shaker. Add the ice and shake for 10 to 15 seconds.

4. Strain the cocktail into a rocks glass filled with fresh ice. Top with soda water and garnish with a thyme bundle.

Bar Tip: 1. If you are not able to find fresh Concord grapes for the syrup, you can use 2 cups store-bought Concord grape juice instead; simmer the syrup until it is reduced by about half. 2. Don't know what to do with leftover syrup? Embrace the fall chill and pour it over some vanilla or coconut milk ice cream for a delicious, indulgent treat.

BEAM BULLDOG

This cocktail pays homage to Jacob and Catharine Beam who founded the town of Beamsville—the place we call home—after immigrating to Canada in 1788. A spirit-forward cocktail, it shows off the flavour complexity of the amaro, vermouth, and rye. The green cardamom pods used in the syrup impart a lighter, less smoky flavour than black cardamom would, allowing notes of citrus and mint to rise to the surface. The result is a highly aromatic cocktail that smells as nice as it tastes.

FOR THE CARDAMOM SYRUP (MAKES ABOUT ½ CUP, ENOUGH FOR 48 COCKTAILS)

¼ cup granulated sugar

¼ cup water

2 green cardamom pods

FOR THE COCKTAIL

2 ounces rye whisky

¾ ounce sweet vermouth

½ ounce amaro

½ teaspoon cardamom syrup

2 dashes peach bitters

Handful of ice cubes

Grapefruit peel, for garnish

1. Make the cardamom syrup. Combine the sugar, water, and cardamom pods in a small pot and heat over medium heat, stirring occasionally until the sugar has dissolved. Remove the pot from the heat and let the cardamom pods steep in the mixture until it has cooled to room temperature.

2. Strain the syrup into an airtight container. The syrup will keep in the refrigerator for up to 2 weeks.

3. Place a square wine glass in the freezer to chill at least 1 hour before you plan to serve the cocktail.

4. Make the cocktail. Add the whisky, vermouth, amaro, syrup, and bitters to a mixing glass. Add the ice and stir for 30 seconds.

5. Strain the cocktail into the chilled wine glass and garnish with grapefruit peel.

Bar Tip: 1. Before you put the final citrus garnish on the drink, twist the citrus peel over the glass to release the fruit's oils and increase the scent and flavour of the cocktail. 2. Use the leftover cardamom syrup to make your spring-time Whisky Sour (page 44) appropriate for sweater weather by adding ¼ ounce before shaking. The syrup is also great drizzled over a slice of sponge cake or some vanilla or coconut ice cream.

TRUE CANADIAN

Quite possibly one of the most patriotic cocktails we have ever crafted, using quintessential Canadian ingredients: fresh-pressed apple cider, maple syrup, and spirits handcrafted in Canada. It doesn't get much better than that. The sweet maple syrup and cider pair well with the spicy rye whisky, resulting in a perfectly balanced cocktail with just the right amount of warmth from the bitters. And did you know that Canada produces nearly 80% of the world's maple syrup? That makes us pretty lucky, if you want our humble opinion!

3 cups fresh-pressed apple cider

1½ cups rye whisky

3 tablespoons pure maple syrup
    (No. 1 Medium grade)

30 dashes aromatic bitters

8 handfuls of ice cubes

8 dehydrated apple slices (page 250),
    for garnish

1. Add the apple cider, rye whisky, maple syrup, and bitters to a pitcher. Stir to combine.

2. Fill 8 rocks glasses with ice, and divide the cocktail evenly among them. Garnish each glass with a slice of dehydrated apple.

Bar Tip: This cocktail is also great served warm while enjoying a picnic on a crisp fall day. Simply warm the apple cider and maple syrup in a medium pot over low heat. Add 1½ ounces rye whisky and a few dashes of bitters to each glass before topping with the warm cider mixture.

VESPÈRE

One of the biggest supporters of our distillery in Montreal is our friend Maximiliano Vallée Valletta, of Les Enfants Terribles. This cocktail is his spin on the classic Vesper, traditionally crafted with dry gin, vodka, and Lillet Blanc. With the addition of elderflower liqueur and apple juice, this cocktail has the perfect balance of sweetness and fruit aroma, which is complemented by the star anise.

1 ounce vodka

¾ ounce gin

½ ounce apple juice

½ ounce elderflower liqueur

3 dashes pear bitters

1 whole star anise, more for garnish

Handful of ice cubes

Grapefruit peel, for garnish

1. Add the vodka, gin, apple juice, elderflower liqueur, bitters, and star anise to a mixing glass. Add the ice and stir for 20 to 30 seconds.
2. Strain the cocktail into a coupe glass. Garnish with star anise and grapefruit peel.

THE REBOUND DATE

— MAKES 1 COCKTAIL —

This cocktail is full of amazing flavour, thanks to the sea buckthorn tonic syrup and the punch of citrus and juniper from the gin. It is so wonderful, in fact, that Jacob Wharton-Shukster, of Restaurant Chantecler in Toronto, won the Dillon's Cocktail Cup with it. Sea buckthorns are naturally very tart, so this is not a sweet cocktail, yet it is a finely balanced drink that any cocktail enthusiast is sure to enjoy. Depending on where you live, sea buckthorns may be tricky to source, but you can always order them online.

FOR THE SEA BUCKTHORN TONIC SYRUP

½ ounce sea buckthorn juice
    (about 15 berries; see Bar Tip)
1 ounce Artisan Tonic Syrup (page 243)
½ ounce simple syrup (page 240)

FOR THE COCKTAIL

1½ ounces dry gin
1 ounce sea buckthorn tonic syrup
½ ounce yellow Chartreuse
½ ounce fresh lemon juice
5 dashes hops bitters
Handful of ice cubes, more for serving
1 ounce soda water
Sea buckthorn berries, for garnish

1. Make the sea buckthorn tonic syrup. Add the sea buckthorn juice, Artisan Tonic Syrup, and simple syrup to a jar and stir to combine.

2. Make the cocktail. Add the gin, syrup, yellow Chartreuse, lemon juice, and bitters to a cocktail shaker. Add the ice and shake for 10 to 15 seconds.

3. Fill a highball glass with fresh ice cubes and strain the cocktail into the glass. Top with soda water and garnish with sea buckthorn berries.

Bar Tip: To extract the juice from the sea buckthorns, combine them with ¼ cup water in a small pot and cook over medium heat until the berries have burst and broken down, about 5 minutes. Let the mixture cool. Purée in a blender until smooth. Pour the purée into a cheesecloth-lined fine-mesh sieve and let the juice drain into a bowl until you have the required amount.

SPICED PEAR FIZZ

— MAKES 8 COCKTAILS —

A quintessential fall cocktail recipe. Shortly after opening the distillery, we spent an afternoon picking pears with friends at a local farm and after all that hard work, and baskets of beautiful pears, we needed a drink. This cocktail is an ode to that crisp afternoon in the orchard. It is the perfect blend of warm spices and fresh fruit. The Spiced Pear Fizz would make a great addition to any festive fall get-together.

FOR THE PEAR PURÉE
(MAKES ABOUT 2 CUPS,
ENOUGH FOR 10 COCKTAILS)
....

4 pears, peeled and cored (Bosc or
    Bartlett pears work best)
3 ounces fresh lemon juice
1 tablespoon fresh rosemary leaves

FOR THE ROSEMARY AND CLOVE
SYRUP (MAKES ABOUT 2 CUPS,
ENOUGH FOR 10 COCKTAILS)
....

1 cup granulated sugar
1 cup water
2 teaspoons whole cloves
6 fresh rosemary sprigs

FOR THE COCKTAILS
....

12 ounces gin
12 ounces pear purée
6 ounces rosemary and clove syrup
6 ounces fresh lemon juice
16 dashes pear bitters
Handful of ice cubes, more for serving
8 ounces soda water
8 fresh rosemary sprigs and
    8 pear slices, for garnish

1. Make the pear purée. Slice the pears and add them to a blender along with the lemon juice and rosemary. Blend on high speed until smooth. Gently strain the mixture through a fine-mesh sieve.

2. Make the rosemary and clove syrup. Combine the sugar, water, cloves, and rosemary in a pot and bring to a boil, stirring until the sugar has dissolved. Remove the pot from the heat and let stand for 30 minutes.

3. Strain the syrup into an airtight jar. The syrup can be stored in the refrigerator for up to 2 weeks.

4. Make the cocktail. Add the gin, pear purée, syrup, lemon juice, and bitters to a large mason jar. Add the ice, cover with the lid, and shake vigorously for 10 to 15 seconds.

5. Fill 8 highball glasses or rocks glasses with fresh ice cubes and strain the cocktail into the glasses. Top each glass with soda water, and garnish with rosemary and a pear slice.

Bar Tip: We suggest straining the pear purée before using it, but if you want to achieve a more viscous cocktail, you can skip that step and shake the drink for a few more seconds to incorporate the purée into the cocktail.

APPLE ROSEMARY RICKEY

— MAKES 1 COCKTAIL —

In this fall spin on the good old Rickey cocktail, we take some liberties by omitting the traditional gin or bourbon in favour of orange liqueur. The combination of herbal and citrus flavours works so well to conjure that fall feeling.

2 sweet apple slices, more for garnish

1 fresh rosemary sprig, another for garnish

2 ounces orangecello or orange liqueur of choice

1 ounce fresh lime juice

2 dashes ginger bitters

Handful of ice cubes, more for serving

3 ounces soda water

1. Add the apple slices and rosemary sprig to a cocktail shaker and muddle until the apples are pulpy and the rosemary is fragrant.

2. Add the orangecello or orange liqueur, lime juice, and bitters. Add the ice and shake for 10 to 15 seconds.

3. Fill a highball glass with fresh ice cubes. Double-strain the cocktail into the glass to ensure there are no lingering rosemary leaves. Top with the soda water and garnish with apple slices and a rosemary sprig.

Through the Flower

If there was ever a cocktail to share with friends, this is it. This recipe was contributed by Evelyn Chick, of Pretty Ugly Bar in Toronto, where shared cocktails are a staple on the menu. This drink combines an array of spirits, each with its own distinctive flavours. The rose gin and schnapps both bring sweetness, while the verjus and lemon juice balance it out with their clean and crisp acid notes.

4½ ounces Dillon's Rose Gin or liqueur-style gin of choice

4½ ounces white port

4 ounces dry gin

1½ ounces peach schnapps

1 ounce water

¾ ounce verjus (see Bar Tip)

½ ounce fresh lemon juice

1. Add the gin, port, schnapps, water, verjus, and lemon juice to a small pot. Heat the mixture to 150°F, making sure it does not come to a boil.
2. Transfer the mixture to a teapot or similar serving vessel. Pour each cocktail into a heatproof snifter glass or its own tea cup and serve warm.

Bar Tip: Verjus is a juice pressed from grapes harvested very early in the season, with bright flavours and crisp acidity that add intense fruit accents to the recipe. It can also be made by pressing other fruits such as crab apples with added flavourings like lemon, sorrel, or spices. Look for it at specialty food shops or online.

Paper Plane

This cocktail features a timeless combination of rich spirits and clean acidity that is so appropriate for the fall. The ingredients are bar staples, and they're all measured in equal parts, which makes it an easy cocktail to craft. The most challenging part of this recipe might be folding up a mini paper plane to use for garnish!

¾ ounce rye whisky

¾ ounce Aperol

¾ ounce amaro

¾ ounce fresh lemon juice

2 dashes orange bitters

Handful of ice cubes

Mini paper airplane, for garnish
(optional)

1. Add the whisky, Aperol, amaro, lemon juice, and bitters to a cocktail shaker. Add the ice and shake for 10 to 15 seconds.

2. Strain the cocktail into a coupe glass. Garnish with a paper plane, if desired.

WHITE RUSSIAN 2.0

— MAKES 1 COCKTAIL —

We have taken the classic White Russian, a 1960s signature cocktail, and added a little twist. Instead of using heavy cream, we opt for nut milk. We use almond milk here, but feel free to experiment with whatever type of nut milk you prefer. This makes for a slightly lighter cocktail, and the almond milk adds the perfect amount of nutty flavour, which pairs extremely well with the coffee and chocolate notes from the bitters.

FOR THE COFFEE SYRUP
(MAKES 1 CUP, ENOUGH
FOR 8 COCKTAILS)

½ cup water

½ cup granulated sugar

2 teaspoons ground coffee

FOR THE COCKTAIL

Handful of ice cubes

2 ounces vodka

1 ounce coffee syrup

1 ounce unsweetened almond
    or other nut milk

2 dashes chocolate bitters

1. Make the coffee syrup. Combine the water, sugar, and coffee in a small pot and bring to a boil. Reduce the heat to a simmer, stirring occasionally until the sugar has dissolved, 2 to 3 minutes. Remove the pot from the heat and let cool for at least 1 hour.

2. Strain the syrup through an ultra-fine-mesh sieve or coffee filter. The syrup will keep in an airtight container in the refrigerator for up to 2 weeks.

3. Make the cocktail. Fill a rocks glass with ice. Add the vodka, syrup, milk, and bitters. Stir to combine.

ROSEMARY MAPLE PECANS

— MAKES 2 CUPS —

Here's a nibble that you just can't stop eating, no matter how hard you try! These maple and rosemary pecans are a great treat to serve during cocktail hour. They are also a welcome addition to any cheese and charcuterie board (page 131).

2 tablespoons butter

1 teaspoon sea salt

Heaping ¼ teaspoon freshly
    ground pepper

2 cups pecan halves

3 fresh rosemary sprigs

¼ cup maple syrup
    (No. 1 Medium grade)

1. Preheat the oven to 325°F and line a baking sheet with parchment paper.

2. Melt the butter in a small pot over medium heat. Add the salt and pepper.

3. Place the nuts in a medium bowl and add the butter mixture, rosemary sprigs, and maple syrup. Toss to coat the nuts evenly.

4. Spread the nuts on the baking sheet. Bake for 20 to 30 minutes, until toasted.

Kitchen Tip: We leave the rosemary sprigs whole, but you can also roughly chop the leaves and sprinkle them across the pecans before placing them in the oven.

FIG AND GOAT CHEESE PROSCIUTTO CUPS

These little prosciutto cups are the perfect appetizer for any cocktail party and feature a fall favourite—figs. Right around this time of year, sweet, plump fresh figs grace the aisles of pretty much every grocery store. Their honey-like sweetness is the perfect accompaniment to the salty richness of the prosciutto. Enjoy these alongside a Paper Plane (page 175), a Figgin' Love You (page 143), or a Beam Bulldog (page 160).

12 thin slices prosciutto

¾ cup soft goat cheese

2 fresh thyme sprigs, leaves removed
    and chopped

3 fresh figs, stemmed and cut
    into quarters

Liquid pure honey, for drizzling

Sea salt

1. Preheat the oven to 425°F and grease a mini muffin tin with butter or non-stick cooking spray.

2. Press a prosciutto slice into each muffin cup so it covers the bottom and sides. Bake for 8 to 10 minutes, or until crisp. Let cool for 20 minutes before removing from the muffin tin.

3. In a small bowl, stir together the goat cheese and thyme.

4. Place 1 tablespoon of the goat cheese mixture in the bottom of each cup and top each cup with a fig quarter. Drizzle with honey and finish with a generous sprinkle of sea salt.

SAVOURY PEAR TART

— SERVES 10 TO 12 —

Not only do we love making cocktails with pears when they are in season, but this pear tart is yet another way to enjoy that fall fruit favourite. The fresh lemon and the orange bitters accent the sweet, juicy pears perfectly. This treat is a great way to either start or end a relaxing evening. For a sweet pairing, enjoy it with the Spiced Pear Fizz (page 168) or No Fixed Address (page 136).

½ (1-pound/450 g) package puff pastry, thawed

2 Bartlett pears, cored and thinly sliced

1 tablespoon lemon zest

2 tablespoons fresh lemon juice

3 dashes orange bitters

½ teaspoon sea salt

½ teaspoon freshly ground pepper

¾ cup grated Pecorino Romano cheese

½ cup crushed walnuts

¼ cup flat-leaf parsley, chopped

1. Preheat the oven to 450°F and line a baking sheet with parchment paper.

2. Roll out one sheet of puff pastry into an 11- x 14-inch rectangle and transfer to the baking sheet. Pierce the surface with a fork and place in the freezer for 15 minutes.

3. In a bowl, combine the pear slices, lemon zest, lemon juice, bitters, salt, and pepper. Toss to coat evenly.

4. Sprinkle the puff pastry evenly with the cheese, leaving a 1-inch border around the edge. Arrange the pear slices over the cheese. Bake for 15 to 20 minutes, until the pastry is golden and puffed.

5. Top the tart with the walnuts and parsley. Cut into squares and serve immediately.

SPICY AND SWEET CHARRED BRUSSELS SPROUTS

— SERVES 4 —

This recipe is a riff on a dish we first enjoyed in Montreal and quickly became obsessed with recreating at home. Brussels sprouts are so versatile in the ways they can be prepared. Roasting them is by far one of our favourite ways to enjoy them, and tossed in this sweet and spicy sauce, they are the perfect addition to your pre-dinner snack menu. Serve them alongside a Weekend in Niagara (page 140) cocktail or even a classic Manhattan (page 151).

1½ pounds Brussels sprouts

2 tablespoons extra-virgin olive oil

Kosher salt

3 tablespoons liquid pure honey

1 tablespoon Sriracha sauce

1 tablespoon fresh lime juice

3 dashes lime bitters

2 tablespoons pine nuts

1. Preheat the oven to 400°F and line a baking sheet with parchment paper.

2. Cut off the stems of the Brussels sprouts and remove any yellow outer leaves. Cut large sprouts in half so all the sprouts are similar in size.

3. Place the Brussels sprouts in a large bowl, drizzle with the olive oil, and season generously with kosher salt. Toss to coat.

4. Arrange the Brussels sprouts in a single layer on the baking sheet. Roast for 35 to 40 minutes, until they are crisp and golden brown on the outside and tender on the inside. Shake the pan a few times during the cooking to ensure the sprouts don't burn.

5. Meanwhile, whisk together the honey, Sriracha sauce, lime juice, and bitters in the same large bowl previously used. Season with kosher salt.

6. Transfer the Brussels sprouts to the large bowl and sprinkle with pine nuts. Toss lightly to coat. Transfer to a serving bowl and serve immediately.

WINTER

Winter marks the shift to dark spirits and warm cocktails. After time spent outdoors, whether you're skating, snowshoeing, or just running to the car, it's nice to come home to a drink that will take away the chill. Spirit-forward cocktails like a Martinez (page 205) or a Sazerac (page 218) take precedence this time of year, thanks to their bold flavours and tummy-warming effects. There may be less fresh, local fruit available during the winter months, but there are still some great options to bring in fruit flavour, such as cranberries in a Cranberry Crush (page 209), pomegranates in a Pomegranate and Ginger Spritzer (page 193), and winter citrus in drinks like a Blood Orange Sparkling Mule (page 221). The holidays also mean more entertaining and party shenanigans. We know how busy the holiday season can be, so we have included some easy-to-craft but still super-impressive cocktails—like the Holiday Pomegranate Punch (page 222)—that are sure to please the crowds and ease your stress levels.

COCKTAILS

SNACKS

WINTER NEGRONI

....

— MAKES 1 COCKTAIL —

Blood orange and rosemary might be one of our favourite winter flavour combinations. Here, those flavours help transform one of our favourite warm-weather drinks into a cocktail perfect for a cozy winter day spent inside. The egg white gives the cocktail more weight and a richer texture, but if you aren't a fan of cocktails with egg whites, you can omit it or use aquafaba instead.

1½ ounces fresh blood orange juice

½ teaspoon granulated sugar

1 fresh rosemary sprig, another
    for garnish

2 ounces dry gin

2 ounces Campari

1 ounce sweet vermouth

1 egg white (or 1 ounce aquafaba;
    see Bar Tip)

2 dashes orange bitters

Handful of ice cubes

1. Add the blood orange juice, sugar, and rosemary to a cocktail shaker. Muddle until the rosemary starts to break down and become fragrant. Add the gin, Campari, vermouth, egg white or aquafaba, and bitters.

2. Remove the spring portion of a Hawthorne strainer and drop the spring into the shaker. Shake with vigour for 1 minute. Add the ice and shake again for at least another minute.

3. Strain the cocktail into a rocks glass and garnish with a rosemary sprig.

Bar Tip: Aquafaba is the liquid in a can of chickpeas or the liquid left in the pot after you cook dried chickpeas. It acts as an emulsifier and a foaming agent in the same way that egg white does. If you're vegan or just a little put off by the idea of there being raw egg in your cocktail, aquafaba will allow you to make traditional sours or fizzes without ever cracking an egg. Don't worry about the smell or taste of the aquafaba; the smell will evaporate, and the chickpea taste will be neutralized when you shake the cocktail.

TURM ME UP TEA

Tea is a great addition to many cocktails, and this spice-infused tea is no exception. The bold Middle Eastern flavours from the turmeric and cinnamon give this cocktail a rich aroma and a different taste, while the fresh lemon juice brightens up the finish.

FOR THE CINNAMON AND TURMERIC TEA (MAKES 4 CUPS, ENOUGH FOR 10 COCKTAILS)

4 cups water

2 tea bags (orange pekoe works best)

2 (3-inch) cinnamon sticks, broken into smaller pieces

1 (2-inch) piece fresh turmeric root, sliced

FOR THE COCKTAIL

3 ounces cinnamon and turmeric tea

1 ounce vodka

¼ ounce fresh lemon juice

2 dashes ginger bitters

Handful of ice cubes, more for serving

Cinnamon stick, for garnish

1. Make the cinnamon and turmeric tea. Bring the water to a boil and pour it into a teapot. Add the tea bags, cinnamon sticks, and turmeric. Let the mixture steep for 10 minutes.

2. Strain the tea through a fine-mesh sieve into a mason jar. Let cool. The tea will keep at room temperature for up to 3 days.

3. Make the cocktail. Add the tea, vodka, lemon juice, and bitters to a cocktail shaker. Add the ice and shake for 10 to 15 seconds.

4. Strain the cocktail into a rocks glass filled with fresh ice cubes. Garnish with a cinnamon stick.

Bar Tip: Get creative with your cocktail garnishes. Try lighting the end of the cinnamon stick with a match to smoke the cinnamon. Not only does it smell amazing, but you will be sure to impress your pals with your top-notch garnish skills.

POMEGRANATE AND GINGER SPRITZER

— MAKES 1 COCKTAIL —

Pomegranate and ginger pack an incredible punch of flavour that's especially welcome in the winter when we all have a case of the winter blues. The sweetness and subtle hint of spice from the syrup marry with the little kick of clove and cinnamon from the bitters in this holiday-ready cocktail. If you're tempted to tinker, gin would be a great base spirit to use in place of the vodka, as would Ginger Beer (page 246 or store-bought) in place of the soda water if you really want to knock that ginger flavour out of the park!

FOR THE POMEGRANATE AND GINGER SYRUP (MAKES ABOUT 1 CUP, ENOUGH FOR 4 COCKTAILS)

1 cup fresh pomegranate juice
    (2 to 3 pomegranates; see Bar Tip)
⅓ cup granulated sugar
2 teaspoons fresh lime juice
1 (2-inch) piece fresh ginger, thinly sliced

FOR THE COCKTAIL

2 ounces pomegranate and ginger
    syrup
1 ounce vodka
2 dashes aromatic bitters
Handful of ice cubes, more for serving
1 ounce soda water
Pomegranate arils, for garnish

1. Make the pomegranate and ginger syrup. Combine the pomegranate juice, sugar, lime juice, and ginger in a small pot and bring to a boil. Reduce the heat and simmer for 5 to 8 minutes, until the liquid begins to thicken slightly, periodically pressing the ginger with the back of a spoon to help bring out its flavour.

2. Remove the pot from the heat and let cool for 30 minutes. Strain the syrup through a fine-mesh sieve into an airtight container. The syrup will keep in the refrigerator for up to 2 weeks.

3. Make the cocktail. Add the syrup, vodka, and bitters to a cocktail shaker. Add the ice and shake for 10 to 15 seconds.

4. Strain the cocktail into a highball glass filled with fresh ice cubes. Top with soda water and garnish with pomegranate arils.

Bar Tip: 1. To make the pomegranate juice, remove the arils. (Cut the fruit in half crosswise, turn each half over, and give them several good whacks with a wooden spoon.) Add the arils to a blender and blend on high speed until all the arils are broken, about 30 seconds. Strain the mixture through a fine-mesh sieve into a bowl, pressing the solids with the back of a spoon to help extract all the juice. The juice can be stored in an airtight container in the refrigerator for up to 5 days. 2. For a non-alcoholic cocktail, enjoy 1 ounce of the syrup with 4 ounces of soda water. The syrup is also great drizzled over a slice of sponge cake.

EGGNOG

It wouldn't be winter without a nice tall glass of eggnog, especially around the holidays. With this recipe devised by one of our very own team members, we are setting you up to be the hero of the party with the best 'nog around. Like many traditional eggnog recipes, this one calls for the mixture to spend 2 weeks in the refrigerator to fully marry all the flavours together, so be sure to keep that in mind if you're planning to serve this rich seasonal treat for a special occasion.

12 pasteurized eggs, separated

1 cup + 3 tablespoons granulated sugar

6⅓ cups whole milk

3 cups heavy (35%) cream

1½ cups rye whisky

1 tablespoon freshly grated nutmeg,
    more for garnish

1 tablespoon pure vanilla extract

Splash of aged rum

1. In the bowl of a stand mixer, beat the egg yolks until they lighten in colour. Gradually beat in 1 cup of the sugar until it is fully incorporated and the mixture is thick and pale.

2. Remove the bowl from the mixer. Add the milk, cream, rye whisky, nutmeg, vanilla, and rum. Stir by hand to combine, then transfer the mixture to a large bowl.

3. Wash and dry the mixer bowl, then beat the egg whites until small peaks start to form. Add the remaining 3 tablespoons sugar and beat until stiff peaks form.

4. Whisk the egg whites into the yolk mixture until fully incorporated. Pour the eggnog into airtight jars and store in the refrigerator for 2 weeks before drinking.

5. Shake each jar for a few seconds before pouring the eggnog into a snifter glass or a rocks glass. Garnish with freshly grated nutmeg.

RED WINE SOUR

If you want to impress your pals with a cool-looking cocktail, this is the one to serve. Floating the red wine on the top of the whisky and lemon mixture gives the drink a striking look that is pretty impressive, and is actually fairly easy to achieve. You can thank us later. You may also be surprised that we suggest adding whisky, lemon, and red wine to the same cocktail, but don't be scared. Though each flavour is strong on its own, they blend well together—we promise.

2 ounces rye whisky

1 ounce fresh lemon juice

1 ounce simple syrup (page 240)

2 dashes aromatic bitters

Handful of ice cubes, more for serving

1 ounce medium-bodied dry red wine

1. Add the rye whisky, lemon juice, syrup, and bitters to a cocktail shaker. Add the ice and shake for 10 to 15 seconds.

2. Strain the cocktail into a rocks glass filled with fresh ice cubes.

3. Hold a spoon just above the surface of the cocktail with the back facing up. Gently pour the wine over the spoon so that it floats on top of the cocktail.

The Elder Orange Fizz

— Makes 1 cocktail —

Gin and elderflower liqueur is a combination you can never go wrong with. And adding almost any pop of flavour to those two ingredients always seems to make magic. The Ginger Beer and fresh blood orange juice in this cocktail amplify the floral notes of the elderflower liqueur, and the Ginger Beer gives it a spicy finish. If ginger beer isn't your thing, replace it with soda water for all of the fizz without the extra kick.

2½ ounces Ginger Beer (page 246; see Bar Tip)

1 ounce dry gin

¾ ounce elderflower liqueur

½ ounce fresh lime juice

Handful of ice cubes

1 ounce fresh blood orange juice

2 dashes orange bitters

Fresh or dehydrated blood orange slice (page 250) and fresh thyme sprig, for garnish

1. To a rocks glass, add the Ginger Beer, gin, elderflower liqueur, and lime juice. Top the glass with ice cubes.
2. Slowly pour in the orange juice. Add the bitters. Stir to combine. Garnish with a blood orange slice and a thyme sprig.

Bar Tip: If you don't have a batch of your own homemade Ginger Beer on hand, and don't have time to make some, any non-alcoholic ginger beer from the market will do the trick here—so no pressure.

Traditional Absinthe Service

Absinthe can be used in some pretty iconic cocktails, among them the Sazerac (page 218) and Corpse Reviver #2 (page 217), but it can also be enjoyed on its own. Here are the steps to enjoy a traditional absinthe service with the fountain, glasses, and a whole lot of fun. While many people believe that adding sugar to their absinthe is a must, it really comes down to personal preference. With the complexity of flavour and clean, smooth finish found in Dillon's own absinthe, we don't usually recommend adding sugar. But the choice is yours.

PER GLASS

1½ ounces absinthe
Sugar cube (optional)
Ice water

1. Fill the reservoir of an absinthe fountain with ice and water.
2. Measure the absinthe into each glass.
3. Position a glass under the water spout. If desired, place an absinthe spoon with a sugar cube on it above the glass. Slowly drip ice-cold water over the sugar (or straight into the glass).
4. Once the spirit has turned milky white (called louching), turn off the spout and enjoy.

Bar Tip: If you don't have an absinthe fountain at home, slowly pouring ice-cold water into your absinthe will achieve the same effect. A liquid measuring cup or carafe will help control the amount of water added. The best louching results are achieved when you have a ratio of about 1 part absinthe to 2 to 4 parts water.

KIR ROYALE

The perfect brunch starter cocktail that couldn't be any easier to craft. Thanks to the rich flavour and vibrant colour of the black currants used to make cassis, this classic takes the elegance and fun factors up a few notches. Since most cassis is quite sweet, use a nice dry sparkling wine for this recipe. Anything with its own residual sugar will make the cocktail too sweet.

½ ounce cassis or crème de cassis

3 ounces dry sparkling wine

Lemon peel, for garnish

1. Add the cassis to a flute glass. Top with the sparkling wine. Garnish with a lemon peel.

Bar Tip: Peel the lemon using a vegetable peeler. For added elegance, twist the peel around a wooden spoon handle and hold for about 20 seconds to get an impressive curl in the peel.

MARTINEZ

Here's our take on the classic Martinez. Unlike its predecessor, the Martini, the Martinez is crafted with sweet vermouth instead of dry. The maraschino liqueur changes the flavour profile too, giving a hint of cherry flavour. Feel free to mix up some of our suggestions below for a version of this drink that is truly your own.

2 ounces dry gin

¾ ounce sweet vermouth

¼ ounce maraschino liqueur

2 dashes orange bitters

Handful of ice cubes

Orange peel, for garnish

1. Add the gin, vermouth, maraschino liqueur, and bitters to a mixing glass. Add the ice and stir for 20 to 30 seconds.
2. Strain the cocktail into a coupe glass and garnish with an orange peel.

Bar Tip: If you're interested in a variation on our Martinez recipe, try one of the following: replace the maraschino liqueur with orange liqueur; use an aromatic-style bitters in place of the orange bitters; garnish with a lemon twist instead of the orange peel.

BOULEVARDIER

If you like a Negroni, you should definitely give this cocktail a try. Using rye whisky in place of gin gives a woodsy, barrel-aged flavour, which is complemented by the sweetness of the vermouth and the bitterness of the Campari. We add a few dashes of coffee bitters to round out the flavour, but you can go the more traditional route and use an aromatic bitters, if you prefer.

1½ ounces rye whisky

¾ ounce Campari

¾ ounce sweet vermouth

2 or 3 dashes coffee bitters

Handful of ice cubes

1 (2-inch-square) ice cube, for serving

Whisky-Soaked Cherry (page 249),
    for garnish

1. Add the rye whisky, Campari, vermouth, and bitters to a mixing glass. Add the ice cubes and stir for 20 to 30 seconds.

2. Strain the cocktail into a rocks glass over a large ice cube. Garnish with a Whisky-Soaked Cherry.

CRANBERRY CRUSH

....

— MAKES 8 COCKTAILS —

The fresh cranberries and whole black peppercorns used in the shrub offer a well-balanced mix of spice and tart notes, which makes this cocktail taste like the most festive aspects of winter and the holiday season. If you replace the gin with vodka, you'll find yourself with a more natural and less sweet version of a vodka cranberry.

FOR THE CRANBERRY AND PEPPER SHRUB (MAKES 2 CUPS, ENOUGH FOR 16 COCKTAILS)

....

1 cup filtered water

2 tablespoons black peppercorns

2 cups fresh cranberries

1 cup apple cider vinegar

½ cup liquid pure honey (see Bar Tip)

FOR THE COCKTAILS

....

1 cup dry gin

1 cup cranberry and pepper shrub

16 dashes cranberry bitters

Handful of ice cubes, more for serving

1 cup soda water

Fresh cranberries and black peppercorns, for garnish

1. Make the cranberry and pepper shrub. Combine the water and peppercorns in a medium pot and bring to a boil. Reduce the heat to a simmer. Add the cranberries and continue to simmer for 10 minutes, or until the cranberries are completely broken down and the liquid is bright red.

2. Remove the pot from the heat and stir in the cider vinegar and honey. Let cool to room temperature.

3. Strain the shrub through a fine-mesh sieve into an airtight jar. The shrub will keep in the refrigerator for up to 2 weeks.

4. Make the cocktail. Add the gin, shrub, and bitters to a large mason jar. Add the ice, seal the lid, and shake for 10 to 15 seconds.

5. Fill 8 rocks glasses with fresh ice, then divide the cocktail evenly among them. Top each glass with 1 ounce of soda water and garnish with cranberries and black pepper.

Bar Tip: Maple syrup can be used in place of honey as the sweetener in the shrub recipe above, if desired. We suggest substituting the honey with ½ cup No. 1 Medium grade maple syrup.

WINTER SIDECAR

— MAKES 1 COCKTAIL —

By adding a rosemary honey syrup to this classic cocktail, we've created a cool-weather variation. Classically made with Cognac, a grape-based brandy produced only in France, we use brandy in this recipe.

FOR THE ROSEMARY HONEY SYRUP (MAKES ABOUT ½ CUP, ENOUGH FOR 16 COCKTAILS)

¼ cup water
¼ cup liquid pure honey
1 fresh rosemary sprig

FOR THE COCKTAIL

1½ ounces brandy
¾ ounce Cointreau or orange liqueur of choice
¾ ounce fresh lemon juice
¼ ounce rosemary honey syrup
Handful of ice cubes
Dehydrated lemon wheel (page 250), for garnish

1. Make the rosemary honey syrup. Combine the water, honey, and rosemary in a small pot and bring to a simmer, stirring until the honey has dissolved. Remove the pot from the heat and let cool to room temperature.

2. Remove the rosemary sprig and transfer the syrup to an airtight container. The syrup can be stored in the refrigerator for up to 2 weeks.

3. Place a coupe glass in the freezer to chill at least 1 hour before you plan to serve the cocktail.

4. Make the cocktail. Add the brandy, Cointreau, lemon juice, and syrup to a cocktail shaker. Add the ice and shake for 10 to 15 seconds.

5. Strain the cocktail into the chilled coupe glass and garnish with a dehydrated lemon wheel.

HOT TODDY

With a cocktail as well-known as a hot toddy, there are so many variations available to you. Whisky, brandy, or rum all work well as the spirit base; black tea can be used in place of hot water for an earthier twist; and if you are looking to make the drink even more seasonal, replace the tea with hot apple cider, or incorporate some fresh cranberries as a garnish.

1 tea bag (Earl Grey or orange pekoe)

1 tablespoon liquid pure honey

1½ ounces rye whisky

½ ounce fresh lemon juice

Lemon wheel and cinnamon stick,
    for garnish

1. Bring at least 2 cups of water to a boil. Pour 4 ounces into a small teapot, add the tea bag, and let steep for 3 to 5 minutes.

2. Pour the remaining boiling water into a mug or heatproof snifter glass. Once the glass is warm, dump the water out and coat the bottom of the mug or glass with the honey.

3. Add the rye whisky, lemon juice, and steeped tea. Stir. Garnish with a lemon wheel and a cinnamon stick.

SQUEEZE ME CLEMMIE

— MAKES 8 COCKTAILS —

The crisp and refreshing taste of fresh clementine juice never fails to conjure that holiday feeling. In this cocktail, the vodka marries all kinds of fresh citrus flavours, but the sweet tang of the clementine is what shines through. And wouldn't this just look lovely displayed with a bowl of fresh clementines next to it as part of your holiday soiree. We think so!

1 cup vodka

¾ ounce limoncello

3 cups fresh clementine juice

½ cup fresh lemon juice

½ cup simple syrup (page 240)

Bucket of ice cubes, for serving

8 dehydrated clementine wheels
    (page 250), for garnish

1. Add the vodka, limoncello, clementine juice, lemon juice, and syrup to a pitcher or glass drink dispenser with a spigot. Stir to combine. Chill in the refrigerator until it is time to enjoy.

2. Set out a display of elegant stemmed wine glasses and an ice bucket filled with ice cubes, and allow guests to serve themselves. Have the dehydrated clementine wheels in a dish on the side for garnish.

Bar Tip: A splash of pomegranate juice would be a fun addition to change the colour and add even more depth of flavour to this seasonal cocktail.

CHERRY GIN CORPSE REVIVER #2

— MAKES 1 COCKTAIL —

We've always been big fans of the classic version of this cocktail but thought it time to liven it up a bit and add more depth of flavour with an unexpected addition. Where the original calls for dry gin, we use Dillon's Cherry Gin. This drink is spirit forward and packs a kick, and the combination of cherry and anise is a pleasant surprise.

1 ounce Dillon's Cherry Gin or dry gin of choice

1 ounce fresh lemon juice

1 ounce Cointreau or orange liqueur of choice

1 ounce Lillet Blanc

1 bar spoon absinthe

Handful of ice cubes

Orange peel, for garnish

1. Place a coupe glass in the freezer to chill at least 1 hour before you plan to serve the cocktail.

2. Add the gin, lemon juice, Cointreau, Lillet Blanc, and absinthe to a cocktail shaker. Add the ice and shake for 10 to 15 seconds.

3. Strain the cocktail into the chilled coupe glass and garnish with orange peel.

SAZERAC

Hailing from New Orleans, the Sazerac is a variation of the old-fashioned and was made with French brandy before bartenders gradually switched to rye whisky. It is one of the few cocktails in which absinthe is used, but even with its minor role in this cocktail, it gives a knock-out performance. Used only as a wash for the glass, it leaves behind anise and grapefruit notes that complement and balance the rye and bitters like no other. Bravo!

1 brown sugar cube

2½ ounces rye whisky

2 dashes Peychaud's Bitters

1 dash aromatic bitters

Handful of ice cubes, more for serving

1 bar spoon absinthe

Lemon peel, for garnish

1. In a mixing glass, muddle the sugar cube with a few drops of water. Add the rye whisky, Peychaud's Bitters, aromatic bitters, and ice. Stir for 20 to 30 seconds.

2. Add the absinthe to a rocks glass and swirl it around until the inside is evenly coated. Discard the excess absinthe.

3. Strain the cocktail into the rocks glass and add fresh ice, if desired. Garnish with lemon peel.

BLOOD ORANGE SPARKLING MULE

— Makes 1 cocktail —

The Moscow Mule isn't just a summertime cocktail anymore! Dress it up with some winter citrus and a splash of bubbly wine and enjoy this refreshing cocktail all year round. If blood oranges aren't available, replace them with navel oranges or grapefruit. Making this cocktail is also a great reason to bust out those beautiful copper mugs you put away at the end of the summer.

1 ounce vodka

1 ounce fresh blood orange juice

1 ounce fresh lime juice

2 dashes orange bitters

Handful of ice cubes, more for serving

2 ounces Ginger Beer (page 246; see Bar Tip)

1 ounce dry sparkling wine

Fresh mint and a dehydrated blood orange wheel (page 250), for garnish

1. Add the vodka, blood orange juice, lime juice, and bitters to a cocktail shaker. Add the ice and shake for 10 to 15 seconds.

2. Strain the cocktail into a copper cup filled with fresh ice cubes. Add the Ginger Beer and top with sparkling wine. Garnish with mint and a dehydrated blood orange wheel.

Bar Tip: If you don't have a batch of your own homemade Ginger Beer on hand, and don't have time to make some, any non-alcoholic ginger beer from the market will do the trick here—so no pressure.

HOLIDAY POMEGRANATE PUNCH

— MAKES 8 COCKTAILS —

In the winter, it's not often that you enjoy fresh and bright-tasting cocktails. This one has all the summery lightness that orange and lemon and citrus bring, with more traditional winter flavours of pomegranate juice and sweet apple cider. This cocktail can also be served as a warm punch on an extra-chilly day. To make the warm version, pour the ingredients listed in step 1 (except the gin) into a pot and bring to a simmer. Add 1 ounce of the gin to each glass and top with the warm juice mixture. Leave out the sparkling wine and garnish with an orange slice instead of the pomegranate arils.

1 cup fresh pomegranate juice (about 2 pomegranates; see Bar Tip)

1 cup dry gin

1 cup fresh orange juice

¾ cup fresh-pressed apple cider

2 tablespoons fresh lemon juice

1 (25-ounce/750 mL) bottle dry sparkling wine

15 dashes orange bitters

Orange slices, for garnish

Arils from 1 pomegranate, for garnish

1. Add the pomegranate juice, gin, orange juice, apple cider, and lemon juice to a punch bowl or glass drink dispenser with a spigot. Stir to combine. Place the mixture in the refrigerator to chill for at least 1 hour.

2. When you're ready to serve, remove the bowl or dispenser from the refrigerator and slowly add the sparkling wine and bitters. Gently stir to combine. Float orange slices on top.

3. Serve in stemmed wine glasses, and top each glass with a sprinkling of pomegranate arils.

Bar Tip: 1. To make the pomegranate juice, remove the arils. (Cut the fruit in half crosswise, turn each half over, and give them several good whacks with a wooden spoon.) Add the arils to a blender and blend on high speed until all the arils are broken, about 30 seconds. Strain the mixture through a fine-mesh sieve into a bowl, pressing the solids with the back of a spoon to help extract all the juices. The juice can be stored in an airtight container in the refrigerator for up to 5 days. 2. If you're having a gathering, make the punch well in advance so you have one less thing to think about when it's party time. To ensure your punch tastes bubbly and fresh, don't add the sparkling wine until the last minute.

AVIATION

The beautiful purple hue that this drink takes on thanks to the crème de violette definitely makes it a showstopper. Crème de violette, or liqueur de violette, is a liqueur with violet flower flavouring and colouring that is crafted from brandy, a neutral spirit base, or both. The taste and aroma are distinctly floral and sweet. The classic Aviation recipe calls for a cherry as the garnish, but a pretty lemon twist works well too. We serve this cocktail in a chilled vintage wine glass, but a Martini glass would also work well.

1½ ounces dry gin

¾ ounce Luxardo maraschino liqueur

½ ounce fresh lemon juice

¼ ounce crème de violette

Handful of ice cubes

Fresh sweet cherry and lemon peel,
    for garnish

1. Place a vintage wine glass in the freezer to chill at least 1 hour before you plan to serve the cocktail.

2. Add the gin, maraschino liqueur, lemon juice, and crème de violette to a cocktail shaker. Add the ice and shake for 10 to 15 seconds.

3. Strain into the chilled wine glass. Spear a cherry with a cocktail pick and use for garnish alongside the lemon peel.

GHOST ORCHARD

— MAKES 1 COCKTAIL —

Kevin Delaney, of the bar Brux House in Hamilton, Ontario, believes low-alcohol cocktails can and should still be packed with flavour. He crafted this one so that it has an abundance of aromatics, thanks to the cider and fennel syrup and the many complex notes in the vermouth. Fresh lemon juice gives this drink the perfect balance of sweet and tart flavour.

FOR THE CIDER AND FENNEL
SYRUP (MAKES ABOUT 2 CUPS,
ENOUGH FOR 16 COCKTAILS)
·················

2 cups chopped fennel
1 cup dry cider
¾ cup granulated sugar

FOR THE COCKTAIL
·················

2 ounces sweet vermouth
1 ounce cider and fennel syrup
1 ounce fresh lemon juice
Handful of ice cubes, more for serving
Fresh sweet cherry and fennel frond,
    for garnish

1. Make the cider and fennel syrup. Combine the fennel, cider, and sugar in a medium pot and bring to a boil. Reduce the heat and simmer for 5 minutes.

2. Transfer the mixture to a heatproof container with a lid and let the syrup steep with the fennel for at least 24 hours in the refrigerator.

3. Strain the syrup using a fine-mesh sieve. The syrup can be kept in an airtight container in the refrigerator for up to 2 weeks.

4. Make the cocktail. Add the vermouth, syrup, and lemon juice to a cocktail shaker. Add the ice and shake for 10 to 15 seconds, until the shaker is cold to the touch.

5. Strain the cocktail into a rocks glass filled with fresh ice cubes. Garnish with a cherry and a fennel frond.

THE BRANDY 105

Inspired by the classic French 75 recipe, which calls for gin and sparkling wine, we decided to try using a barrel-aged fruit spirit instead. This cocktail embraces the winter with its hearty, rich, and less sweet flavours. We use aromatic bitters in this recipe, but you could always try this cocktail with orange bitters, or cranberry bitters for an even more wintery feel.

1½ ounces brandy

½ ounce fresh lemon juice

3 dashes aromatic bitters

Handful of ice cubes

3 ounces dry champagne
	or sparkling wine

Lemon peel, for garnish

1.	Add the brandy, lemon juice, and bitters to a cocktail shaker. Add the ice and shake for 10 to 15 seconds.

2.	Strain the cocktail into a flute glass and top with champagne or sparkling wine. Use a zester to pull a thin strip of lemon peel for garnish.

ROASTED CRANBERRY FLATBREADS

— Makes 2 flatbreads; serves 8 to 10 —

If this pizza-like appetizer doesn't get you into the holiday spirit, then nothing will. The goat cheese, cranberries, thyme, and maple syrup result in a delight of holiday flavours in every bite. Perfect for your next holiday party, especially when served with a bubbly and vibrant cocktail like a Kir Royale (page 202) or a cocktail with a stronger backbone like a Boulevardier (page 206).

1½ cups fresh cranberries

3 tablespoons pure maple syrup
(No. 1 Medium grade)

1 tablespoon finely chopped shallots

1 teaspoon chopped fresh thyme,
divided

¼ teaspoon sea salt

6 dashes cranberry bitters

2 soft flatbreads or naan breads,
10 to 12 inches in length

1 cup soft goat cheese

1. Preheat the oven to 375°F.

2. Add the cranberries, maple syrup, shallots, half of the thyme, the salt, and the bitters to an 8-inch square baking dish. Toss to combine. Roast for about 15 minutes, stirring once or twice, until the cranberries burst and the mixture starts to bubble and caramelize along the edges.

3. Remove the dish from the oven and stir until the cranberries are broken down and the mixture is thick and chunky.

4. Lay the flatbreads out on a work surface. Spread the hot cranberry mixture over the flatbreads, dividing it evenly and spreading it close to the edges. Evenly sprinkle the goat cheese across each flatbread.

5. Bake the flatbreads directly on the oven rack until the cheese is softened and the flatbread is crispy, 8 to 10 minutes.

6. Transfer to a cutting board and sprinkle with the remaining thyme. Cut into wedges or strips and serve warm.

Blackberry-Topped Brie

A big wheel of baked Brie never really goes out of style, does it? The possibilities are endless when it comes to toppings, but we're partial to a combination of dark berries, ginger, and nuts. Over the years of baking Brie wheels, we've learned a few tricks. One is to slice a thin layer off the top of the Brie before baking it to allow all that gooey goodness inside to fully melt. It also creates a perfect little cup for the toppings to rest in. This baked Brie would be great alongside a Brandy 105 (page 229) or Red Wine Sour (page 197).

2 cups fresh blackberries, more for garnish

1 tablespoon fresh lemon juice

1 tablespoon liquid pure honey

1 teaspoon pure vanilla extract

2 dashes ginger bitters

1 (7- to 8-ounce) wheel of Brie, at room temperature

Handful of raw pecan halves

Fresh thyme leaves, for garnish (optional)

Crackers, for serving

1. Preheat the oven to 350°F and line a baking sheet with parchment paper.

2. In a medium pot, combine the blackberries, lemon juice, honey, vanilla, and bitters. Heat over medium heat, stirring regularly. As the berries begin to release their juice, turn the heat up to medium-high. Cook for about 10 minutes, stirring periodically, until the mixture starts to reduce and the liquid is syrupy.

3. Carefully cut the top rind off the Brie wheel and discard. Place the Brie on the baking sheet and bake for 15 minutes or until melted through.

4. Top with the blackberry compote, pecans, fresh blackberries, and thyme leaves, if desired. Serve immediately with a selection of your favourite crackers.

MINI GRILLED CHEESE SLIDERS

— MAKES 15 MINI SANDWICHES —

These mini grilled cheese sandwiches make us so nostalgic for our childhood, but no one ever said a grown-up couldn't enjoy a crispy, cheese-filled sandwich from time to time. They're cute, they're hand-held, they're customizable, and they are absolutely delicious! We've kept the recipe simple and leave it up to you to make these sandwiches your own or tailor them to the tastes of your guests. These would make a great pairing with a Sazerac (page 218) to balance their richness or even a festive Cranberry Crush (page 209).

1 baguette

3 to 4 tablespoons unsalted butter

1 cup grated aged Gouda cheese

2 cups arugula

1 teaspoon chili flakes

Freshly ground black pepper

Sea salt

Tomato chutney, for serving (optional)

Bacon jam, for serving (optional)

1. Thinly slice the baguette into 30 (½-inch) slices.

2. Butter one side of each of the baguette slices and arrange them buttered side down. Divide the cheese evenly among 15 of the slices. Top with the arugula. Sprinkle with chili flakes, and season with black pepper and sea salt. Top with the remaining baguette slices, buttered side up this time.

3. Heat a large frying pan over medium-low heat. Grill the sandwiches in batches for 3 to 4 minutes on each side, or until the cheese starts to melt and the bread is golden brown and crispy.

4. Arrange the sandwiches on a platter and serve alongside bowls of tomato chutney and/or bacon jam, if desired.

Kitchen Tip: In addition to the arugula, feel free to add other ingredients to the sandwiches. Try them with caramelized onions or tomatoes, and experiment with different cheeses, such as Brie or an aged blue cheese.

TOMATO AND OLIVE TAPENADE

— MAKES 1 CUP —

A tapenade like this is easy to prepare ahead of time and the perfect light offering to kick off a winter-themed dinner party. We use black olives in this recipe, but green olives or a combination of both would be just fine too. The salty component of the tapenade offsets the deeper, richer cocktail flavours that you will find in something like a Martinez (page 205) or Ghost Orchard (page 226).

1 cup oil-cured pitted black olives, drained

½ cup oil-packed sun-dried tomatoes, sliced

¼ cup coarsely chopped flat-leaf parsley

2 tablespoons extra-virgin olive oil

2 tablespoons fresh lemon juice

1 tablespoon drained capers

2 teaspoons fresh thyme leaves

1 garlic clove, crushed

4 or 5 dashes aromatic bitters

Freshly ground black pepper

1 baguette, sliced (for serving)

1. In a food processor or blender, combine the olives, sun-dried tomatoes, parsley, oil, lemon juice, capers, thyme, garlic, and bitters. Whirl until finely chopped, stopping to scrape down the sides if needed.

2. Scrape the tapenade into a small serving bowl and season with black pepper. Serve alongside baguette slices. The tapenade will keep in an airtight container in the refrigerator for up to 1 week.

HANDCRAFTED COCKTAIL STAPLES

One of the most creative and personalized ways to bring complexity and flavour to your cocktails is by adding a homemade element. In this section, we've included recipes for the syrups, garnishes, and other ingredients that we find ourselves making again and again. Whether you decide to make your own simple syrup (page 240), Artisan Tonic Syrup (page 243), or garnish of Whisky-Soaked Cherries (page 249), your guests will appreciate the extra love you've put in by creating your own cocktail ingredients and accoutrements. Of course, if you find yourself short on time—some require preparation in advance—you can always source them from local shops and specialty food stores instead.

SYRUPS AND SHRUBS

Throughout the book, you will find cocktails that call for simple syrup, an infused syrup, or a shrub. Regular simple syrup brings sweetness, but adding infused syrups or shrubs to a cocktail is a simple and effective way not only to add sweetness but also to deepen flavour. They also provide an opportunity to get creative with your drinks and bring in seasonal flavours. If a recipe calls for a peach syrup but you think you would prefer blueberry flavour because blueberries are in season, make the change! We encourage you to experiment and have fun with building your cocktails.

A shrub is a concentrated syrup that combines fruit, sugar, and vinegar. The result is a sweet and acidic syrup that can impart a tart flavour to a drink's profile. Thanks to the acidity from the vinegar, using a shrub in a cocktail can also virtually eliminate the need for fresh lemon or lime juice. Often, fresh herbs and spices are infused in the shrub to create more interesting and deeper flavour combinations. Making your own shrub is very easy and the flavour possibilities are endless.

SIMPLE SYRUP

— MAKES ABOUT 1½ CUPS —

Most cocktail recipes that require some added sweetness call for a simple syrup. Using simple syrup allows you to control the sweetness you add to a cocktail. Because the recipe for simple syrup uses a 1:1 ratio, you can easily make as large or as small a batch as you need.

1 cup granulated sugar

1 cup water

1. Combine the sugar and water in a small pot and heat over medium-high heat, stirring occasionally until the sugar has fully dissolved.
2. Remove the pot from the heat and let cool to room temperature.
3. Transfer the syrup to an airtight container. The syrup will keep in the refrigerator for up to 2 weeks.

RICH SYRUP

— MAKES ABOUT 1 CUP —

Rich syrup is a variation on simple syrup that uses more sugar to yield a richer mixture. It is made in the same way as simple syrup, but uses a 2:1 ratio of sugar to water. Many bartenders and home cocktail enthusiasts prefer to use rich syrup in cocktails because of its thicker texture, which can add more body and mouthfeel to a drink. Experiment with both to see which one you prefer.

2 cups granulated sugar

1 cup water

1. Combine the sugar and water in a small pot and heat over medium-high heat, stirring occasionally until the sugar has fully dissolved.
2. Remove the pot from the heat and let cool to room temperature.
3. Transfer the syrup to an airtight container. The syrup will keep in the refrigerator for up to 2 weeks.

HONEY SYRUP

....

— MAKES 1 CUP —

Using honey in place of granulated sugar is a great option if you'd prefer a syrup that is less processed and more natural. The quality and flavour of the honey will affect the overall flavour of the syrup, and because honey is more viscous, the syrup will be thicker in consistency, giving cocktails a richer mouthfeel and texture than simple syrup. We suggest using a mild flavoured, local honey to give your cocktails a special flavour.

1 cup liquid pure honey

1 cup water

1. Combine the honey and water in a medium pot and bring to a boil over medium-high heat, stirring until the honey is fully incorporated.
2. Remove the pot from the heat and let cool to room temperature.
3. Transfer the syrup to an airtight container. The syrup will keep in the refrigerator for up to 2 weeks.

AGAVE SYRUP

....

— MAKES 1 CUP —

Agave syrup will lend a bit of colour to your cocktail, but it is perfect for making vegan-friendly drinks. Keep in mind that agave is 1.5 times sweeter than sugar, so when you use agave syrup in place of simple syrup, be sure to cut the amount the recipe calls for by half.

1 cup agave syrup

1 cup water

1. Combine the agave syrup and water in a small pot and heat over medium-high heat, stirring until the agave is fully incorporated.
2. Remove the pot from the heat and let cool to room temperature.
3. Transfer the syrup to an airtight container. The syrup will keep in the refrigerator for up to 2 weeks.

INFUSED SYRUP

— MAKES 1½ CUPS —

Infused syrups bring more flavour to your cocktail without the need to add or muddle additional ingredients. Syrups can be infused with a wide range of ingredients—anything from rosemary or cloves, to fresh fruit, to warm, rich spices like cinnamon. Throughout the book, we use many infused syrups.

1 cup granulated sugar

1 cup water

Infusion fruit(s), spice(s),
        and/or herb(s) of choice

1. Combine the sugar, water, and your chosen fruit(s), spice(s), and/or herb(s) in a small pot and heat over medium-high heat, stirring occasionally until the sugar has fully dissolved.

2. Remove the pot from the heat and let cool to room temperature. If using fruit, press on the fruit with the back of a spoon to extract as much flavour as possible.

3. Strain the syrup through a fine-mesh sieve into an airtight container. The syrup will keep in the refrigerator for up to 2 weeks.

Bar Tip: Our rule of thumb when adding fresh fruit to a syrup is to use 1 cup of chopped fruit for every 1 cup of water. When using herbs or spices, we use a handful and taste as the syrup cools, adjusting the steeping time to achieve the desired amount of flavour.

ARTISAN TONIC SYRUP

— MAKES ABOUT 2 CUPS —

There are a lot of handcrafted tonic waters or syrups on the market that you can use to top off a gin and tonic, but if you want to give making your own syrup a whirl, we find this recipe particularly tasty. It takes roughly 24 hours to prepare the syrup, but once it is made it will keep for up to 3 months in the refrigerator.

3 cups water

¼ cup orange zest

¼ cup lemon zest

¼ cup orange peel

¼ cup lemon peel

1 tablespoon ground cassia bark

1 tablespoon ground coriander

1 tablespoon dried juniper berries

1 (4-inch) stick licorice root,
    roughly broken up

1¾ cups granulated sugar

1 ounce vodka

¼ teaspoon ground cinchona bark

1. In a medium pot, combine the water, orange and lemon zest and peel, cassia bark, coriander, juniper berries, and licorice root. Bring to a boil, then add the sugar, stirring until it has dissolved. Remove the pot from the heat and let the syrup cool to room temperature.

2. Strain the syrup into an airtight jar.

3. Meanwhile, in a separate small jar, combine the vodka and ground cinchona bark. Let steep for at least 2 hours or overnight if possible.

4. Strain the infused vodka through a coffee filter into a third airtight jar.

5. Add 1½ ounces of the vodka and cinchona tincture to the syrup and stir to combine. The tonic syrup will keep in the refrigerator for up to 3 months.

Bar Tip: When using tonic syrup in your cocktails, remember that you will still need to add soda water for carbonation. You may want to experiment with the ratio of syrup to soda water, but we suggest 1 ounce syrup for every 3 ounces soda water you use.

SHRUB

There are two basic ways to make a shrub. The first, which we call the hot method, uses heat to speed up the diffusion of flavour into the syrup. It is the best method to use when time is of the essence. The second way to make a shrub is the cold method. It can be used when you have more time. The cold method has the benefit of allowing all the freshness of the ingredients to remain intact. The fruits and herbs or spices you use will vary depending on the flavour you wish to incorporate into your cocktails. See the chart on the opposite page for ideas of fruits and herbs you can use to infuse your homemade shrub, and the amount of each fruit and/or herb you'll need based on the recipes below.

HOT METHOD

1 cup granulated sugar

1 cup water

Fresh fruit of choice (see chart on
    opposite page for measurements)

Fresh herbs of choice (optional)

1 cup apple cider vinegar

1. Combine the sugar and water in a small pot and heat over medium-high heat, stirring until the sugar has dissolved.
2. Add the fruit and herbs, if desired. Bring to a boil, then reduce the heat and simmer for 2 to 3 minutes.
3. Remove the pot from the heat and let the mixture cool to room temperature.
4. Strain out the solids using a fine-mesh sieve. Pour the shrub into a clean airtight jar. Add the vinegar and stir. The shrub will keep in the refrigerator for up to 2 weeks.

COLD METHOD

1 cup apple cider vinegar

Fresh fruit of choice (see chart on
    opposite page for measurements)

Fresh herbs of choice (optional)

1 cup granulated sugar

1. Combine the vinegar, fruit, and herbs (if using) in a jar with an airtight seal. Seal the jar and shake vigorously for about 20 seconds.
2. Allow the fruit to infuse at room temperature for about 3 days, giving the jar a vigorous shake once or twice each day.
3. Strain out the solids through a sieve lined with a double layer of cheesecloth. Pour the liquid into a clean airtight jar.
4. Add the sugar, seal the jar, and shake until the sugar is completely dissolved. Add additional sugar and vinegar to taste. The shrub will keep in the refrigerator for up to 1 week.

FRUITS AND VEGETABLES	AMOUNT	FRESH HERBS AND OTHER INGREDIENTS	AMOUNT
Stone fruits, chopped (e.g., peaches, plums, cherries)	2 cups	Fresh basil	1 cup
		Fresh rosemary	½ cup
Berries	2 cups	Fresh thyme	¼ cup
Rhubarb, chopped	3 cups	Fresh lavender	1 to 2 tablespoons
Vegetables, chopped (e.g., cucumbers, beets, fennel)	2 cups	Fresh ginger, thinly sliced	½ cup

GINGER BEER

— MAKES 8 CUPS —

Although there is nothing wrong with using store-bought ginger beer in your cocktail creations, you really can't replace that homemade flavour. Besides, we always think it's fun to get your hands dirty and prepare some of your ingredients from scratch. Having freshly crafted ginger beer on hand is great for those times when you want a refreshing drink but without the alcohol. Thanks to the fresh lemon juice, this ginger beer has a nice acidic finish, which is balanced perfectly by the spiciness of the fresh ginger. The active dry yeast boosts the fermentation; it's the same yeast you find in the baking section of your supermarket. You can also use yeast from a make-your-own wine or beer shop.

9 cups water, divided

¼ cup peeled and grated fresh ginger

¼ cup fresh lemon juice

½ teaspoon baking powder

2 cups organic cane sugar

1 teaspoon active dry yeast

Bar Tip: If you store the ginger beer in glass bottles, they may crack or explode as a result of pressure buildup during fermentation. That's why we recommend using plastic bottles with screw tops.

1. Pour 4 cups of the water into a large pot. Add the ginger, lemon juice, and baking powder. Bring the mixture to a boil, then reduce to a simmer. Add the cane sugar and stir until it has dissolved.

2. Add the remaining 5 cups water. Remove the pot from the heat and allow the liquid to cool to room temperature.

3. Stir in the yeast, then cover the pot with a clean kitchen towel. Place the pot in a dark place and let sit at room temperature for 3 hours.

4. Strain the liquid through a fine-mesh sieve into a pitcher. Transfer to 2 clean 1-quart plastic pop bottles with an airtight closure (or more smaller bottles), leaving at least an inch of headspace at the top. Securely close the bottles and leave the ginger beer to ferment in a warm, dark room for 2 to 3 days. At least once and ideally 3 times a day, carefully loosen and then retighten the caps, without fully opening each bottle. This will relieve some of the pressure that builds up during the fermentation process.

5. Once the ginger beer has finished fermenting (the plastic bottles should feel hard and you shouldn't be able to make a dent in the plastic when you press on it), store it in the refrigerator with the lids tightly fastened. It will keep for up to 2 weeks.

CLARIFIED TOMATO WATER

— Makes 8½ cups —

Just what you need to make a vegan Dillon's Caesar (page 120). By using only the strained juices of the tomatoes, cucumber, and celery, your finished cocktail will be clear in colour—a fun spin on the classic Canadian drink.

4 pounds very ripe heirloom tomatoes, cored and cut into quarters

½ pound unpeeled English cucumber cut into chunks

1 large celery stalk, cut into 2-inch pieces

2 tablespoons finely grated fresh horseradish (optional)

Kosher salt

Freshly ground black pepper

Granulated sugar

1. Purée the tomatoes, cucumbers, celery, and horseradish in a blender until smooth.

2. Line a fine-mesh sieve with cheesecloth and set it over a large bowl. Pour the purée into the sieve and let the tomato water drain, without stirring or pressing on the solids, for about 2 hours. You should collect at least 3 cups of liquid.

3. Season the tomato water with salt, pepper, and sugar.

Quick Pickled Onions

Enjoy pickled onions as a garnish on a Classic Martini (page 39), or make them to share on a Cheese and Charcuterie Board (page 131) with a Whisky Sour (page 44) in hand. This recipe would also work well with heirloom carrots or green beans. Use them to garnish a Dillon's Caesar (page 120) or simply enjoy them as a snack!

8 ounces pearl onions (about 16), trimmed and peeled

½ cup granulated sugar

½ cup white wine vinegar

½ cup water

½ teaspoon salt

½ teaspoon red peppercorns

2 black cardamom pods

4 fresh thyme sprigs

1. Bring a medium pot of salted water to a boil. Add the onions and cook for 2 minutes. Immediately drain the onions, fill the pot with cold water, and drain again. Transfer the onions to a small bowl to cool. Once the onions are cool enough to handle, place them in a mason jar.

2. In the pot that was used to cook the onions, combine the sugar, white wine vinegar, water, salt, peppercorns, cardamom, and thyme. Bring to a boil, stirring until the sugar has dissolved, about 2 minutes.

3. Pour the hot brine (with the spices) over the onions. Let cool to room temperature, uncovered.

4. Seal the jar and refrigerate for at least 1 hour before serving. If unopened, the jar of pickled onions will keep for up to a year in the brine in a cool place. Once opened, keep the jar in the refrigerator for up to 2 months.

WHISKY-SOAKED CHERRIES

The perfect garnish for cocktails like a Manhattan (page 151) or a Whisky Sour (page 44), these cherries can also be enjoyed as a little snack to reward yourself for all the hard work you've done mixing cocktails! They are sure to impress. Not to mention, they would also make a great gift for the cocktail enthusiast in your life.

1 pound sweet cherries, stemmed
    and pitted
½ cup water
½ cup liquid pure honey
1 teaspoon pure vanilla extract
Pinch of nutmeg
Pinch of ground allspice
1 (3-inch) cinnamon stick
1 (3-inch) strip of orange peel
1 cup whisky
10 to 20 dashes aromatic bitters

1. Divide the cherries into 2 clean 16-ounce mason jars. Set aside.

2. In a medium pot, whisk together the water, honey, vanilla, nutmeg, and allspice. Add the cinnamon and orange peel. Bring to a boil and reduce to simmer for 10 minutes. Let cool.

3. Strain the liquid through a fine-mesh sieve into a pitcher. Add the whisky and bitters, and stir. Divide the mixture evenly between each jar of cherries.

4. Secure the lids on the jars, give them a shake, and refrigerate for at least 3 days before using. The cherries will keep in the refrigerator for up to 3 months.

DEHYDRATED FRUIT GARNISHES

Dehydrated pieces of fruit have become extremely popular cocktail garnishes. With a more concentrated aroma and flavour after the water is removed, dehydrated fruit can add complexity to a drink. The garnish also adds a distinctive look that is sure to impress your friends. Fortunately, these garnishes are easy to make at home, whether you have an electric dehydrator or you're using your oven. Once you've done the prep work, dried fruit can be stored for much longer than fresh fruit, so you'll be ready to mix a beautiful and flavourful cocktail at the drop of a hat. Some of our favourite fruits to use as dehydrated garnishes are lemons, limes, blood oranges, strawberries, figs, and apples.

1. Slice your fruit of choice into ¼-inch-thick slices.

2. If using a dehydrator, set the temperature between 125°F and 140°F. Dehydrating at the lower temperature will result in a more evenly dehydrated product, while setting the temp to 140°F will make the process go a bit faster. You will want to keep an eye on the fruit; this method could take as little as 6 to 8 hours or closer to 24 hours, depending on the moisture level of the fruit. Most dehydrators have a timer feature, so you can set it and forget it overnight. The fruit is done when there is no moisture left and the pieces are completely dry to the touch.

3. If using an oven, set the temperature to 150°F and arrange the fruit in a single layer on a parchment-lined baking sheet. Depending on the type of fruit you are dehydrating, you will want to leave it in the oven anywhere from 6 hours (apples, figs, peaches) to 10 hours (citrus). Check on the fruit every hour or so, and flip the fruit a few times during the dehydrating process. You will know the fruit is ready when the fruit slices are completely dry, no longer pliable, and do not stick to the parchment paper.

ACKNOWLEDGMENTS

When we began writing this book, we had no idea how much of ourselves we would pour into it. We knew it was something we had always dreamt of, and joked about, but to have it come to life was slightly overwhelming—in the best way possible. We truly would not have been able to write *Craft Cocktails* had it not been for those around us, supporting and encouraging us throughout this wild journey. And maybe a few cocktails!

Naturally, our thank-yous must begin with the Dillon's team. We would be nothing without the tireless efforts of our amazing crew. You are not only colleagues but family. You have been vital to the success of the distillery, the Dillon's brand, and of course this book. We are forever grateful.

Thank you to our growers and farming partners. Every drop of alcohol we make starts with you. We know who grows our fruit and grain, and we like it that way. Thank you to Volker Storjohann for our rye grain. Every week you ship us your fresh Ontario rye, milled to our exacting standards, and we couldn't do what we do without you. Thank you to grape growers like the Funks, who have been growing some of the best grapes in Niagara for generations and have become such an important part of crafting our vodka and gin. And a special thank you to others, like Torrie Warner, who grows all our black currants, plums, pears, and so much more, just a couple of kilometres from the distillery. To the Tigchelaar family in Vineland, Ontario, thank you for providing all the fresh strawberries we use in our Strawberry Gin and vermouth. Last but not least, the Smith family, owners of Cherry Lane, just a bit farther down the road, have been growing sour cherries since 1907. Our Cherry Gin wouldn't be the same without the historic local flavour you bring.

Thank you to Barry Imber and the team at Insite Design, in Burlington, Ontario. You have been with us since day one, helping us dream up and create this brand that we have all fallen for hard. You have taught us how important our brand and our story are and how to share both. Thank you for ensuring our aesthetic is always on point and our voice is clear.

Thank you, Nataschia Wielink, our amazing photographer and to stylist Carolee Krause. Because of you this book is filled with stunning images. You understood our vision from day one, and never shied away from early mornings spent running around in muddy fields, and never thought twice about hanging out on the tallest ladder to get the perfect shot.

Thank you to the wonderful team at Penguin Random House Canada. You took a chance on us, and our gratitude for that is endless. To publishing director Andrea Magyar, and to our editors, Rachel Brown and Laura Dosky, your guidance throughout this process has been strong and focused, keeping us in check and on time.

Last, a huge shout-out to the bartenders and chefs who not only contributed their recipes and their talents to help elevate our cocktail collection, but also support us and have become an extension of our Dillon's family, sharing our passion for the spirits we craft. Thank you.

From Geoff: To my wife, Whitney, we began this journey together and look how far we've come. From day one, you have supported this dream of mine in every way possible. We've been together for every moment of this roller-coaster ride and there's no one I'd rather be on it with.

From Whitney: Thank you to my husband, Korey. I cherish your patience and love beyond measure. You were my sounding board and my taste taster (actually, maybe you should be thanking me), and I am so lucky to be living this life with you by my side. All my hugs and kisses to my boys, Cooper and Chase. You gave me time and space to work, helped where you could (juicing citrus!), and are truly the best cheering squad a mother could ask for.

INDEX